I began this journal on...

MY
reading
LIFE

created by
ANNE BOGEL

TEN PEAKS PRESS™
EUGENE, OR

Contents

1 Title _____

2 _____

3 _____

4 _____

📖 **Reading Goals** ....

5 _____

6 _____

7 _____

8 _____

9 _____

10 _____

11 _____

12 _____

13 _____

14 _____

15 _____

16 _____

17 _____

18 _____

19 _____

20 _____

21 _____

📖 *Five Ways to Get More out of Your Reading Life* ....

22 _____

23 _____

24 _____

25 _____

26 _____

27 _____

28 _____

29 _____

30 _____

31 _____

32 _____

72 _____

73 _____

74 _____

75 _____

76 _____

77 _____

78 _____

79 _____

80 _____

81 _____

📖 *Tools for the Reading Life* ... 136

82 _____

83 _____

84 _____

85 _____

86 _____

87 _____

88 _____

89 _____

90 _____

91 _____

92 _____

93 _____

94 _____

95 _____

96 _____

97 _____

98 _____

99 _____

100 _____

Books are *knowledge.*
Books are *reflection.*
Books change your *mind.*

— Toni Morrison

Introduction

I'm so excited you're holding this reading journal in your hands. Tracking your reading is one of the best ways I know to improve your reading life, and I firmly believe that when you get more out of your reading life, your whole life is a little bit better.

That's because a good book is more than just a pleasant diversion on a rainy afternoon. Books bring us joy and happiness, food for thought, conversational fodder, vicarious travel and experience, and knowledge to make the world a better place. In short, good books serve as shortcuts to the things that matter most in life.

You can stumble into a good book, but you can't stumble into a great reading life—and that's where this journal comes in. Tracking the books you read (and the books you *want* to read) benefits your reading life in myriad ways. Your reading journal helps you remember what books you have read and what you thought about them. Logging your books in one place, as you're doing here, gives you an opportunity to examine your reading habits over time. When you have your reading history captured in one place, you can see habits and patterns that are hard to perceive up close, day by day, or book by book. When you track your reading, you can zoom out and see the big picture.

If you feel like you've been on a roll lately with choosing good books, your reading log can help you figure out what those books have in common. If you feel like you're in a slump and haven't been reading anything good (or reading anything at all), your reading log can help you determine why. If you're wondering about the diversity of the books you're reading—whether by genre, topic, or author—your reading log has those answers. When a friend asks for a good book recommendation, your reading journal is full of ideas.

I regularly consult my own reading journal—when someone asks me to recommend a good book, when I want to see if I've been skewing lately toward fiction or nonfiction, when I'm compiling a list of recent favorites, or when I'm planning my next few reads.

My hope is that this journal will help you both articulate your reading taste and broaden your literary horizons. The numerous book lists included in these pages feature titles from a diverse assortment of authors, genres, themes, and more. Just as I do on my blog *Modern Mrs Darcy* and podcast *What Should I Read Next?*, I've included a wide array of genres, styles, settings, structures, and other literary characteristics. The authors and characters reflect the world we live in and represent a variety of races, ethnicities, cultures, creeds, and backgrounds. In these ways and more, I've sought to provide a broad range of voices and experiences.

I hope you will find that this reading journal enriches your reading life, inspires you to read more, and is just plain fun to have. Happy reading!

Anne Bogel

Getting Started

- HOW TO USE THIS JOURNAL -

This journal is meant to capture the history of what you've read, to help you reflect on the books you are currently reading, and to help you plan your future reading life.

It's intended to be a tool for your reading life, so don't hesitate to use it like one! Some of us are intimidated by a pristine new book, but I urge you not to let perfectionism hold you back. Get out your favorite pen or pencil, and start writing in it immediately.

This journal is meant to serve you. As you turn the pages, you'll encounter tips to approach your reading life with intention, questions to prompt readerly reflection, and book lists bearing titles you may enjoy reading next. These titles are meant to serve as inspiration; please don't consider these book lists as to-do lists. The goal is not to read every book mentioned here; these lists exist to help you find your next right read. The foundation to a vibrant reading life is a terrific "to be read" list, and this journal will help you capture yours. Don't be afraid to highlight or otherwise annotate the lists of recommended reads included here and to use the "To Be Read" section to capture titles you're interested in reading. Your future self will thank you.

A word about content warnings (sometimes called trigger warnings): Many readers wish to avoid certain kinds of sensitive content or specific triggers. Please know that some of the titles recommended in this journal have tough themes or moments and may include topics that are triggers for some. If you wish to avoid certain themes or topics, I urge you to be kind to yourself by asking your fellow readers and carefully reading reviews to ascertain whether a title is right for you. An online search for "content warnings" pertaining to the title in question may also be helpful; some authors even include them on their websites. These content warnings are meant to help readers avoid being caught off guard by something that will be harmful to them at this time or will otherwise make for a miserable reading experience.

To acquire the habit of reading is to construct for yourself a refuge from almost all the miseries of life.

>>>——»   W. SOMERSET MAUGHAM   «——«<<

- A SNAPSHOT OF MY READING LIFE RIGHT NOW -

What's working in my reading life right now?

_____

_____

_____

_____

_____

_____

Is there anything that's not working?

_____

_____

_____

_____

_____

_____

What are three books I've enjoyed lately?

_____

_____

_____

_____

_____

_____

What have I read lately that didn't work for me?

_____

_____

_____

_____

_____

_____

What do I want to change in my reading life?

_____

_____

_____

_____

_____

_____

What do I want more of in my reading life?

_____

_____

_____

_____

_____

_____

- MY READING HABIT TRACKER -

JAN.	FEB.	MARCH	APRIL	MAY	JUNE
◇	◇	◇	◇	◇	◇
◇	◇	◇	◇	◇	◇
◇	◇	◇	◇	◇	◇
◇	◇	◇	◇	◇	◇
◇	◇	◇	◇	◇	◇
◇	◇	◇	◇	◇	◇
◇	◇	◇	◇	◇	◇
◇	◇	◇	◇	◇	◇
◇	◇	◇	◇	◇	◇
◇	◇	◇	◇	◇	◇
◇	◇	◇	◇	◇	◇
◇	◇	◇	◇	◇	◇
◇	◇	◇	◇	◇	◇
◇	◇	◇	◇	◇	◇
◇	◇	◇	◇	◇	◇
◇	◇	◇	◇	◇	◇
◇	◇	◇	◇	◇	◇
◇	◇	◇	◇	◇	◇
◇	◇	◇	◇	◇	◇
◇	◇	◇	◇	◇	◇
◇	◇	◇	◇	◇	◇
◇	◇	◇	◇	◇	◇
◇	◇	◇	◇	◇	◇
◇	◇	◇	◇	◇	◇
◇	◇	◇	◇	◇	◇
◇	◇	◇	◇	◇	◇
◇	◇	◇	◇	◇	◇
◇	◇	◇	◇	◇	◇
◇	◇	◇		◇	
	◇	◇		◇	

JULY	AUG.	SEPT.	OCT.	NOV.	DEC.
◇	◇	◇	◇	◇	◇
◇	◇	◇	◇	◇	◇
◇	◇	◇	◇	◇	◇
◇	◇	◇	◇	◇	◇
◇	◇	◇	◇	◇	◇
◇	◇	◇	◇	◇	◇
◇	◇	◇	◇	◇	◇
◇	◇	◇	◇	◇	◇
◇	◇	◇	◇	◇	◇
◇	◇	◇	◇	◇	◇
◇	◇	◇	◇	◇	◇
◇	◇	◇	◇	◇	◇
◇	◇	◇	◇	◇	◇
◇	◇	◇	◇	◇	◇
◇	◇	◇	◇	◇	◇
◇	◇	◇	◇	◇	◇
◇	◇	◇	◇	◇	◇
◇	◇	◇	◇	◇	◇
◇	◇	◇	◇	◇	◇
◇	◇	◇	◇	◇	◇
◇	◇	◇	◇	◇	◇
◇	◇	◇	◇	◇	◇
◇	◇	◇	◇	◇	◇
◇	◇	◇	◇	◇	◇
◇	◇	◇	◇	◇	◇
◇	◇	◇	◇	◇	◇
◇	◇	◇	◇	◇	◇
◇	◇	◇	◇	◇	◇
◇	◇	◇	◇	◇	◇
◇	◇	◇	◇	◇	◇
◇	◇	◇	◇	◇	◇
◇	◇	◇	◇	◇	◇
◇	◇	◇	◇	◇	◇
◇	◇	◇		◇	◇
◇	◇				◇

- DIAGNOSE YOUR READING TASTE -

Readers who have satisfying reading lives know what they like and can articulate it, even if only to themselves. Why does this matter? While different readers may share the love of reading, the specific books they love may vary wildly.

I'm not saying there's never a reason to read a book you don't enjoy. Some of the most formative reading experiences, best literary discussions, and most profound personal insights happen with books we *don't* enjoy. (Which is a good thing, because when I was in school, nobody ever asked me if I liked the books I was assigned.) Rather, I *am* saying that when you have a free hour on a Sunday afternoon and you want to curl up in your favorite armchair with a good book, you need to know what kind of book you would actually enjoy reading right then, for the pure pleasure of it.

When you want to read for sheer enjoyment, what kind of books do you turn to? Not the book you *have* to read, or one you feel like you *should* read (or worse, *should* enjoy).

This is the question we need to be able to answer, but it can be surprisingly difficult to do so. When you're trying to identify your reading taste, the following questions may help you put your finger on what makes a book work for you.

What genres do you especially enjoy? Oft-cited options include *historical fiction, mystery, realistic contemporary fiction, science fiction and fantasy, memoir,* and *narrative nonfiction.*

_____

_____

_____

Do you prefer character-driven books that focus on inner transformation or plot-driven books that focus on action and external conflict?

_____

_____

_____

What interests you about a character? Do you need them to be likable? Do you need characters you can root for?

_____

_____

_____

What kind of pacing do you most appreciate? Do you have patience to let a story develop, or do you want strong narrative drive, something that feels more like a page-turner?

_____

_____

_____

_____

Which is more important, a strong plot or beautiful writing?

What topics do you find especially interesting?

What places do you want to vicariously visit?

What are your deal breakers? (We all have topics we don't want to read about. What are yours?)

What is your reading life like right now?

What would you like it to be like?

I have always imagined that *Paradise* will be a kind of library.

— Jorge Luis Borges

Book Lists

- GENRE FAVORITES -

These selections include some of my personal favorite titles in a variety of popular genres. Whether you're confident in your reading taste or exploring what you may enjoy, find your next great read in these genre-specific lists.

HISTORICAL FICTION

These immersive stories take place in the past,
transporting readers to another time and place.

◇ *Code Name Hélène* | Ariel Lawhon

◇ *News of the World* | Paulette Jiles

◇ *Pachinko* | Min Jin Lee

◇ *Dreamland Burning* | Jennifer Latham

◇ *The Good Earth* | Pearl S. Buck

◇ *A Fall of Marigolds* | Susan Meissner

◇ *The Underground Railroad* | Colson Whitehead

◇ *The Tea Girl of Hummingbird Lane* | Lisa See

◇ *Homegoing* | Yaa Gyasi

◇ *Becoming Mrs. Lewis* | Patti Callahan

◇ *The Kite Runner* | Khaled Hosseini

◇ *The Guernsey Literary and Potato Peel Pie Society* |
Annie Barrows & Mary Ann Shaffer

◇ *Wolf Hall* | Hilary Mantel

◇ *A Constellation of Vital Phenomena* | Anthony Marra

◇ *The Vanishing Half* | Brit Bennett

◇ *The Chosen* | Chaim Potok

◇ *The Gown* | Jennifer Robson

◇ *Deacon King Kong* | James McBride

◇ *Hotel on the Corner of Bitter and Sweet* | Jamie Ford

◇ *Snow Falling on Cedars* | David Guterson

MYSTERY

Enjoy a great story and solve the crime with
these absorbing whodunits.

◇ *What I Saw and How I Lied* | Judy Blundell

◇ *Murder on the Orient Express* | Agatha Christie

◇ *Celine* | Peter Heller

◇ *The Daughter of Time* | Josephine Tey

◇ *American Spy* | Lauren Wilkinson

◇ *Fake ID* | Lamar Giles

◇ *The Sweetness at the Bottom of the Pie* | Alan Bradley

◇ *A Study in Scarlet* | Arthur Conan Doyle

◇ *The Mother-in-Law* | Sally Hepworth

◇ *The Name of the Rose* | Umberto Eco

◇ *Magpie Murders* | Anthony Horowitz

◇ *Salvation of a Saint* | Keigo Higashino

◇ *The Silent Patient* | Alex Michaelides

◇ *Bluebird, Bluebird* | Attica Locke

◇ *The Thursday Murder Club* | Richard Osman

◇ *The Unquiet Dead* | Ausma Zehanat Khan

◇ *The Pelican Brief* | John Grisham

◇ *The Westing Game* | Ellen Raskin

◇ *A Study in Charlotte* | Brittany Cavallaro

◇ *Long Bright River* | Liz Moore

LOVE STORIES

Get lost in a book that puts love front and center with these romance, literary, women's fiction, and young adult selections.

◇ *The City Baker's Guide to Country Living* | Louise Miller

◇ *Now That I've Found You* | Kristina Forest

◇ *Edenbrooke* | Julianne Donaldson

◇ *The History of Love* | Nicole Krauss

◇ *The Blue Castle* | L.M. Montgomery

◇ *To All the Boys I've Loved Before* | Jenny Han

◇ *Venetia* | Georgette Heyer

◇ *Boyfriend Material* | Alexis Hall

◇ *Like Water for Chocolate* | Laura Esquivel

◇ *The Switch* | Beth O'Leary

◇ *Love Lettering* | Kate Clayborn

◇ *The Winter Sea* | Susanna Kearsley

◇ *Sweet Sorrows* | David Nicholls

◇ *Anna and the French Kiss* | Stephanie Perkins

◇ *Act Like It* | Lucy Parker

◇ *The Selection* | Kiera Cass

◇ *Tar Baby* | Toni Morrison

◇ *The Princess Bride* | William Goldman

◇ *Tell Me Three Things* | Julie Buxbaum

◇ *If You Come Softly* | Jacqueline Woodson

FANTASY & SCIENCE FICTION

These inventive and imaginative stories feature incredible world-building, captivating characters, and impossible choices that will have you marveling at their author's creativity.

◇ *Uprooted* | Naomi Novik

◇ *Fahrenheit 451* | Ray Bradbury

◇ *Sleeping Giants* | Sylvain Neuvel

◇ *Daughter of Smoke and Bone* | Laini Taylor

◇ *Lock In* | John Scalzi

◇ *The Extraordinaries* | TJ Klune

◇ *Till We Have Faces: A Myth Retold* | C.S. Lewis

◇ *The Left Hand of Darkness* | Ursula K. Le Guin

◇ *The Name of the Wind* | Patrick Rothfuss

◇ *Girls Made of Snow and Glass* | Melissa Bashardoust

◇ *Piranesi* | Susanna Clarke

◇ *The Graveyard Book* | Neil Gaiman

◇ *Dark Matter* | Blake Crouch

◇ *Gods of Jade and Shadow* | Silvia Moreno-Garcia

◇ *The Ten Thousand Doors of January* | Alix E. Harrow

◇ *Children of Blood and Bone* | Tomi Adeyemi

◇ *The Color of Magic* | Terry Pratchett

◇ *The Invisible Life of Addie LaRue* | V.E. Schwab

◇ *Kindred* | Octavia E. Butler

◇ *The City of Brass* | S.A. Chakraborty

CHILDREN'S BOOKS FOR GROWN-UPS

If you're a reader who knows the joy of reading
for a lifetime—or wants to—this list is for you.

◇ *Anne of Green Gables* | L.M. Montgomery

◇ *El Deafo* | Cece Bell

◇ *Betsy-Tacy* | Maud Hart Lovelace

◇ *From the Mixed-Up Files of Mrs. Basil E. Frankweiler* | E.L. Konigsburg

◇ *Out of My Mind* | Sharon M. Draper

◇ *To Night Owl from Dogfish* | Holly Goldberg Sloan & Meg Wolitzer

◇ *Because of Winn-Dixie* | Kate DiCamillo

◇ *Brown Girl Dreaming* | Jacqueline Woodson

◇ *The Phantom Tollbooth* | Norton Juster

◇ *Flora and Ulysses* | Kate DiCamillo

◇ *Out of the Dust* | Karen Hesse

◇ *The Crossover* | Kwame Alexander

◇ *Island of the Blue Dolphins* | Scott O'Dell

◇ *One Crazy Summer* | Rita Williams-Garcia

◇ *The War That Saved My Life* | Kimberly Brubaker Bradley

◇ *The Vanderbeekers of 141st Street* | Karina Yan Glaser

◇ *Where the Red Fern Grows* | Wilson Rawls

◇ *The Penderwicks* | Jeanne Birdsall

◇ *Flygirl* | Sherri L. Smith

◇ *Some Places More Than Others* | Renée Watson

BIOGRAPHY, AUTOBIOGRAPHY, & MEMOIR

Step into someone else's extraordinary lived
experience with these nonfiction tales.

◇ *Persepolis* | Marjane Satrapi

◇ *West with the Night* | Beryl Markham

◇ *The Color of Water* | James McBride

◇ *Notes of a Native Son* | James Baldwin

◇ *Men We Reaped* | Jesmyn Ward

◇ *Wind, Sand, and Stars* | Antoine de Saint-Exupéry

◇ *Know My Name* | Chanel Miller

◇ *Hourglass* | Dani Shapiro

◇ *The Year of Magical Thinking* | Joan Didion

◇ *Hold Still* | Sally Mann

◇ *When Breath Becomes Air* | Paul Kalanithi

◇ *Brain on Fire: My Month of Madness* | Susannah Cahalan

◇ *Reading Lolita in Tehran* | Azar Nafisi

◇ *Good Talk: A Memoir in Conversations* | Mira Jacob

◇ *Don't Let's Go to the Dogs Tonight* | Alexandra Fuller

◇ *Out of Egypt* | André Aciman

◇ *Heating & Cooling* | Beth Ann Fennelly

◇ *The Diary of a Young Girl* | Anne Frank

◇ *The Light of the World* | Elizabeth Alexander

◇ *Smoke Gets in Your Eyes* | Caitlin Doughty

NARRATIVE NONFICTION

These true stories read like novels, compelling
you to keep those pages turning.

◇ *Just Mercy* | Bryan Stevenson

◇ *Maybe You Should Talk to Someone* | Lori Gottlieb

◇ *Into Thin Air* | John Krakauer

◇ *Ballad of the Whiskey Robber* | Julian Rubinstein

◇ *Seabiscuit: An American Legend* | Laura Hillenbrand

◇ *Killers of the Flower Moon* | David Grann

◇ *Underland* | Robert Macfarlane

◇ *The Perfect Storm* | Sebastian Junger

◇ *Five Days at Memorial* | Sheri Fink

◇ *Behind the Beautiful Forevers* | Katherine Boo

◇ *The Warmth of Other Suns* | Isabel Wilkerson

◇ *The Radium Girls* | Kate Moore

◇ *The Emperor of All Maladies* | Siddhartha Mukherjee

◇ *Packing for Mars* | Mary Roach

◇ *The Secret History of Wonder Woman* | Jill Lepore

◇ *The Boys in the Boat* | Daniel James Brown

◇ *The Wild Trees* | Richard Preston

◇ *Team of Rivals* | Doris Kearns Goodwin

◇ *Hidden Figures* | Margot Lee Shetterly

◇ *The Devil in the White City* | Erik Larson

Book Lists

- SEASONAL SELECTIONS -

Reading with the rhythm of the seasons helps you to narrow your choices and enjoy the atmosphere, no matter the weather. Choose a timely book from these lists and slow down, pay attention, and enjoy the changing world around you.

Winter

We begin each year with a clean slate, and plenty of good intentions. But if you want to *keep* your resolutions, it's time to get serious about forming the right habits. These nonfiction titles, focused on our most common collective resolutions, will help you do just that.

◇ *Brave, Not Perfect* | Reshma Saujani

◇ *Off the Clock* | Laura Vanderkam

◇ *Don't Overthink It* | Anne Bogel

◇ *Big Friendship* | Aminatou Sow & Ann Friedman

◇ *The Power of Habit* | Charles Duhigg

◇ *Wild at Home* | Hilton Carter

◇ *Let Your Life Speak* | Parker J. Palmer

◇ *The Miracle of Mindfulness* | Thich Nhat Hanh

◇ *Daily Rituals* | Mason Currey

◇ *Every Body Yoga* | Jessamyn Stanley

◇ *The Checklist Manifesto* | Atul Gawande

◇ *Cozy Minimalist Home* | Myquillyn Smith

◇ *In the Company of Women* | Grace Bonney

◇ *The Path Made Clear* | Oprah Winfrey

◇ *The Lazy Genius Way* | Kendra Adachi

◇ *This Is Where You Belong* | Melody Warnick

◇ *Emotional Agility* | Susan David

◇ *Braving the Wilderness* | Brené Brown

◇ *Make It Happen* | Lara Casey

◇ *Year of Yes* | Shonda Rhimes

LIVELY BOOKS FOR PLANT LOVERS

Dive into a story full of gardens, flowers, and nature's delights. You don't need a green thumb in order to enjoy any of these titles, but it sure doesn't hurt!

◇ **The Language of Flowers** | Vanessa Diffenbaugh

◇ **Braiding Sweetgrass** | Robin Wall Kimmerer

◇ **Garden Spells** | Sarah Addison Allen

◇ **The Signature of All Things** | Elizabeth Gilbert

◇ **The Forgotten Garden** | Kate Morton

◇ **Purple Hibiscus** | Chimamanda Ngozi Adichie

◇ **The Rose Garden** | Susanna Kearsley

◇ **Lab Girl** | Hope Jahren

◇ **The Well-Gardened Mind** | Sue Stuart-Smith

◇ **The Orchid Thief** | Susan Orlean

◇ **My Garden (Book)** | Jamaica Kincaid

◇ **The Black Tulip** | Alexandre Dumas

◇ **Second Nature** | Michael Pollan

◇ **The Botanist's Daughter** | Kayte Nunn

◇ **A Garden of Marvels** | Ruth Kassinger

◇ **A Memory of Violets** | Hazel Gaynor

◇ **The Overstory** | Richard Powers

◇ **The Way Men Act** | Elinor Lipman

◇ **The Invention of Nature** | Andrea Wulf

◇ **The Secret Garden** | Frances Hodgson Burnett

Summer

Whether set at a bucolic beach or by a threatening sea, the common link between these books is the significance of the water to the story.

◇ *The Summer I Turned Pretty* | Jenny Han

◇ *The Education of Margo Sanchez* | Lilliam Rivera

◇ *Castle of Water* | Dane Huckelbridge

◇ *Grief Cottage* | Gail Godwin

◇ *A Long Petal of the Sea* | Isabel Allende

◇ *Chances Are...* | Richard Russo

◇ *Beach Read* | Emily Henry

◇ *Brighton Rock* | Graham Greene

◇ *Haven Point* | Virginia Hume

◇ *The Shell Seekers* | Rosamunde Pilcher

◇ *Lost Lake* | Sarah Addison Allen

◇ *The Next Great Jane* | K.L. Going

◇ *Gift from the Sea* | Anne Morrow Lindbergh

◇ *The Prince of Tides* | Pat Conroy

◇ *Little Beach Street Bakery* | Jenny Colgan

◇ *To the Lighthouse* | Virginia Woolf

◇ *Sea of Poppies* | Amitav Ghosh

◇ *Maine* | J. Courtney Sullivan

◇ *The Island of Sea Women* | Lisa See

◇ *The Last Train to Key West* | Chanel Cleeton

Fall

If you hate horror but are still up for a spine-chilling read,
these seriously spooky (but not quite scary) books are for you.

◇ *The Thirteenth Tale* | Diane Setterfield

◇ *Rebecca* | Daphne du Maurier

◇ *My Sister, the Serial Killer* | Oyinkan Braithwaite

◇ *The Giver* | Lois Lowry

◇ *The Complete Stories* | Flannery O'Connor

◇ *Wuthering Heights* | Emily Brontë

◇ *The Distant Hours* | Kate Morton

◇ *When Mockingbirds Sing* | Billy Coffey

◇ *And Then There Were None* | Agatha Christie

◇ *A Curious Beginning* | Deanna Raybourn

◇ *We Have Always Lived in the Castle* | Shirley Jackson

◇ *The Martian Chronicles* | Ray Bradbury

◇ *Jane Steele* | Lyndsay Faye

◇ *1984* | George Orwell

◇ *The Turn of the Screw* | Henry James

◇ *Never Let Me Go* | Kazuo Ishiguro

◇ *The Hazel Wood* | Melissa Albert

◇ *The Whispering House* | Elizabeth Brooks

◇ *Among the Shadows* | L.M. Montgomery

◇ *Mexican Gothic* | Silvia Moreno-Garcia

You can never
get a cup of *tea*
large enough or a
book long enough
to suit me.

— C.S. Lewis

My "To Be Read" List

Reading at whim is a wonderful thing. But I never want you to be in the mood for a good book without a clue what that book might be. A healthy "to be read" list ensures that you'll never be left without a book for want of good ideas on what to read next. Capture the pertinent details below, including why you're excited to read each title.

TITLE: _____

AUTHOR: _____ DATE ADDED: _____

WHY: _____

_____

TITLE: _____

AUTHOR: _____ DATE ADDED: _____

WHY: _____

_____

TITLE: _____

AUTHOR: _____ DATE ADDED: _____

WHY: _____

_____

TITLE: _____

AUTHOR: _____ DATE ADDED: _____

WHY: _____

_____

TITLE: _____

AUTHOR: _____ DATE ADDED: _____

WHY: _____

_____

TITLE: _____

AUTHOR: _____ DATE ADDED: _____

WHY: _____

_____

TITLE: _____

AUTHOR: _____ DATE ADDED: _____

WHY: _____

_____

TITLE: _____

AUTHOR: _____ DATE ADDED: _____

WHY: _____

_____

TITLE: _____

AUTHOR: _____ DATE ADDED: _____

WHY: _____

_____

TITLE: _____

AUTHOR: _____ DATE ADDED: _____

WHY: _____

_____

TITLE: _____

AUTHOR: _____ DATE ADDED: _____

WHY: _____

_____

TITLE: _____

AUTHOR: _____ DATE ADDED: _____

WHY: _____

_____

TITLE: _____

AUTHOR: _____ DATE ADDED: _____

WHY: _____

_____

TITLE: _____

AUTHOR: _____ DATE ADDED: _____

WHY: _____

_____

TITLE: _____

AUTHOR: _____ DATE ADDED: _____

WHY: _____

_____

TITLE: _____

AUTHOR: _____ DATE ADDED: _____

WHY: _____

_____

TITLE: _____

AUTHOR: _____ DATE ADDED: _____

WHY: _____

_____

A good book is an event in my life.

>>>——» STENDHAL «——«««

TITLE: _____

AUTHOR: _____ DATE ADDED: _____

WHY: _____

_____

TITLE: _____

AUTHOR: _____ DATE ADDED: _____

WHY: _____

_____

TITLE: _____

AUTHOR: _____ DATE ADDED: _____

WHY: _____

_____

TITLE: _____

AUTHOR: _____ DATE ADDED: _____

WHY: _____

_____

TITLE: _____

AUTHOR: _____ DATE ADDED: _____

WHY: _____

_____

TITLE: _____

AUTHOR: _____ DATE ADDED: _____

WHY: _____
_____

TITLE: _____

AUTHOR: _____ DATE ADDED: _____

WHY: _____
_____

TITLE: _____

AUTHOR: _____ DATE ADDED: _____

WHY: _____
_____

TITLE: _____

AUTHOR: _____ DATE ADDED: _____

WHY: _____
_____

TITLE: _____

AUTHOR: _____ DATE ADDED: _____

WHY: _____
_____

TITLE: _____

AUTHOR: _____ DATE ADDED: _____

WHY: _____

_____

TITLE: _____

AUTHOR: _____ DATE ADDED: _____

WHY: _____

_____

TITLE: _____

AUTHOR: _____ DATE ADDED: _____

WHY: _____

_____

TITLE: _____

AUTHOR: _____ DATE ADDED: _____

WHY: _____

_____

TITLE: _____

AUTHOR: _____ DATE ADDED: _____

WHY: _____

_____

My Reading Log

- BOOKS I'VE READ -

A good reading record is an indispensable tool for a vibrant reading life. Capture one hundred of your own reads on the following pages.

BOOK NO.
....
1

◇ FICTION
◇ NONFICTION

DATE STARTED

DATE FINISHED

My Ratings

◇◇◇◇◇
ENJOYMENT

◇◇◇◇◇
CRAFT

◇◇◇◇◇
OVERALL

I'D RECOMMEND
THIS TO:

Title

AUTHOR:
GENRE: LENGTH:
PUBLISHER: YEAR PUBLISHED:
THEMES:

HOW I DISCOVERED THIS BOOK:

MEMORABLE QUOTES:

THOUGHTS & IMPRESSIONS:

Title

AUTHOR: ....

GENRE: .... LENGTH: ....

PUBLISHER: .... YEAR PUBLISHED: ....

THEMES: ....

HOW I DISCOVERED THIS BOOK:

MEMORABLE QUOTES:

THOUGHTS & IMPRESSIONS:

◇ FICTION

◇ NONFICTION

DATE STARTED

DATE FINISHED

My Ratings

◇◇◇◇◇
ENJOYMENT

◇◇◇◇◇
CRAFT

◇◇◇◇◇
OVERALL

I'D RECOMMEND
THIS TO:

BOOK NO.

3

◇ FICTION
◇ NONFICTION

DATE STARTED

DATE FINISHED

My Ratings

◇◇◇◇◇
ENJOYMENT

◇◇◇◇◇
CRAFT

◇◇◇◇◇
OVERALL

I'D RECOMMEND
THIS TO:

Title

AUTHOR:

GENRE: LENGTH:

PUBLISHER: YEAR PUBLISHED:

THEMES:

HOW I DISCOVERED THIS BOOK:

MEMORABLE QUOTES:

THOUGHTS & IMPRESSIONS:

Title

AUTHOR: ....

GENRE: .... LENGTH: ....

PUBLISHER: .... YEAR PUBLISHED: ....

THEMES: ....

HOW I DISCOVERED THIS BOOK:

MEMORABLE QUOTES:

THOUGHTS & IMPRESSIONS:

BOOK NO.
....
4

◇ FICTION
◇ NONFICTION

DATE STARTED

DATE FINISHED

My Ratings

◇◇◇◇◇
ENJOYMENT

◇◇◇◇◇
CRAFT

◇◇◇◇◇
OVERALL

I'D RECOMMEND
THIS TO:

- READING GOALS -

You may have heard the phrase "you get what you measure." If you're looking for a way to invigorate your reading life, try experimenting with concrete reading goals that keep you accountable, inspire you to read more, and are just plain fun to track. Here are some suggestions to help you set measurable, manageable goals that are right for your reading life.

Read more books. If you're discontent with the number of books you're reading these days, try setting a numerical goal to increase the number of books you complete. Whether that means aiming to read a dozen or a hundred, having a number to shoot for will help you read more. Even if you don't hit your goal, you're likely to read more than you would have without it.

Read more pages. Some readers prefer to set a goal based on pages read instead of the number of books completed. This prevents you from prioritizing shorter books over *War and Peace*.

Read consistently. Your goal could be to build reading into the rhythms of your life. Perhaps you aim to read seven days a week, or maybe five. When you read a little bit at a time, but do it on a regular schedule, the minutes add up. (For motivation and accountability, use the habit tracker on page 12.)

Read more genres. If you tend to gravitate toward one or two specific genres, aim to consciously branch out. (Flip to page 18 to review genre favorites and resolve to read one or two from each genre listed there.)

Become a completist. Resolve to finish the works of an author you love or wish to get acquainted with, whether that's an author of classics like Jane Austen, a historian like Doris Kearns Goodwin, or your favorite contemporary novelist.

Broaden your perspective. Embrace diversity in your reading life by striving to read works written by authors whose race, ethnicity, culture, country, and background differ from your own. Not only will you expand your literary horizons, but you might also gain a new perspective, learn about your neighbor, or challenge your own biases and misperceptions.

Try a challenge. A thoughtfully designed reading challenge, such as the annual Modern Mrs Darcy Reading Challenge, can push you to seek out books you might not otherwise discover, while providing a structure to approach them.

Widen your worldview. Aim to read more works in translation. Fiction—and to a lesser extent, nonfiction—helps us empathize with and understand other people and cultures. When we read only books written in our own language, we miss a crucial opportunity. (For ideas, check out the book list on page 172.)

What a blessing it is to love books.

⟫⟶⟫ ELIZABETH VON ARNIM ⟪⟵⟪

BOOK NO.

5

◇ FICTION
◇ NONFICTION

DATE STARTED

DATE FINISHED

My Ratings

◇◇◇◇◇
ENJOYMENT

◇◇◇◇◇
CRAFT

◇◇◇◇◇
OVERALL

I'D RECOMMEND
THIS TO:

Title

AUTHOR:

GENRE: LENGTH:

PUBLISHER: YEAR PUBLISHED:

THEMES:

HOW I DISCOVERED THIS BOOK:

MEMORABLE QUOTES:

THOUGHTS & IMPRESSIONS:

Title

AUTHOR:

GENRE: LENGTH:

PUBLISHER: YEAR PUBLISHED:

THEMES:

HOW I DISCOVERED THIS BOOK:

MEMORABLE QUOTES:

THOUGHTS & IMPRESSIONS:

BOOK NO.

6

◇ FICTION

◇ NONFICTION

DATE STARTED

DATE FINISHED

My Ratings

◇◇◇◇◇
ENJOYMENT

◇◇◇◇◇
CRAFT

◇◇◇◇◇
OVERALL

I'D RECOMMEND
THIS TO:

BOOK NO.

7

◇ FICTION
◇ NONFICTION

DATE STARTED

DATE FINISHED

My Ratings

◇◇◇◇◇
ENJOYMENT

◇◇◇◇◇
CRAFT

◇◇◇◇◇
OVERALL

I'D RECOMMEND
THIS TO:

Title

AUTHOR:

GENRE: LENGTH:

PUBLISHER: YEAR PUBLISHED:

THEMES:

HOW I DISCOVERED THIS BOOK:

MEMORABLE QUOTES:

THOUGHTS & IMPRESSIONS:

Title

AUTHOR: ....

GENRE: .... LENGTH: ....

PUBLISHER: .... YEAR PUBLISHED: ....

THEMES: ....

HOW I DISCOVERED THIS BOOK:

MEMORABLE QUOTES:

THOUGHTS & IMPRESSIONS:

◇ FICTION

◇ NONFICTION

DATE STARTED

DATE FINISHED

My Ratings

◇◇◇◇◇
ENJOYMENT

◇◇◇◇◇
CRAFT

◇◇◇◇◇
OVERALL

I'D RECOMMEND
THIS TO:

....

....

....

....

BOOK NO.

9

◇ FICTION
◇ NONFICTION

DATE STARTED

DATE FINISHED

My Ratings

◇◇◇◇◇
ENJOYMENT

◇◇◇◇◇
CRAFT

◇◇◇◇◇
OVERALL

I'D RECOMMEND
THIS TO:

Title

AUTHOR:

GENRE: LENGTH:

PUBLISHER: YEAR PUBLISHED:

THEMES:

HOW I DISCOVERED THIS BOOK:

MEMORABLE QUOTES:

THOUGHTS & IMPRESSIONS:

Title

AUTHOR:

GENRE: _____ LENGTH: _____

PUBLISHER: _____ YEAR PUBLISHED: _____

THEMES: _____

HOW I DISCOVERED THIS BOOK:

MEMORABLE QUOTES:

THOUGHTS & IMPRESSIONS:

BOOK NO.
10

◇ FICTION
◇ NONFICTION

DATE STARTED

DATE FINISHED

My Ratings

◇◇◇◇◇
ENJOYMENT

◇◇◇◇◇
CRAFT

◇◇◇◇◇
OVERALL

I'D RECOMMEND
THIS TO:

BOOK NO.

11

◇ FICTION
◇ NONFICTION

DATE STARTED

DATE FINISHED

My Ratings

◇◇◇◇◇
ENJOYMENT

◇◇◇◇◇
CRAFT

◇◇◇◇◇
OVERALL

I'D RECOMMEND
THIS TO:

Title

AUTHOR:

GENRE: LENGTH:

PUBLISHER: YEAR PUBLISHED:

THEMES:

HOW I DISCOVERED THIS BOOK:

MEMORABLE QUOTES:

THOUGHTS & IMPRESSIONS:

Title

AUTHOR: ....

GENRE: .... LENGTH: ....

PUBLISHER: .... YEAR PUBLISHED: ....

THEMES: ....

HOW I DISCOVERED THIS BOOK:

MEMORABLE QUOTES:

THOUGHTS & IMPRESSIONS:

◇ FICTION

◇ NONFICTION

DATE STARTED

DATE FINISHED

My Ratings

◇—◇—◇—◇—◇
ENJOYMENT

◇—◇—◇—◇—◇
CRAFT

◇—◇—◇—◇—◇
OVERALL

I'D RECOMMEND
THIS TO:

BOOK NO.
....
13

◇ FICTION
◇ NONFICTION

DATE STARTED

DATE FINISHED

My Ratings

◇◇◇◇◇
ENJOYMENT

◇◇◇◇◇
CRAFT

◇◇◇◇◇
OVERALL

I'D RECOMMEND
THIS TO:

Title

AUTHOR:

GENRE: .... LENGTH:

PUBLISHER: .... YEAR PUBLISHED:

THEMES:

HOW I DISCOVERED THIS BOOK:

MEMORABLE QUOTES:

THOUGHTS & IMPRESSIONS:

Title

AUTHOR: ....

GENRE: .... LENGTH: ....

PUBLISHER: .... YEAR PUBLISHED: ....

THEMES: ....

HOW I DISCOVERED THIS BOOK:

MEMORABLE QUOTES:

THOUGHTS & IMPRESSIONS:

◇ FICTION

◇ NONFICTION

DATE STARTED

DATE FINISHED

My Ratings

◇◇◇◇◇
ENJOYMENT

◇◇◇◇◇
CRAFT

◇◇◇◇◇
OVERALL

I'D RECOMMEND
THIS TO:

The world
was *hers*
for the
reading.

— Betty Smith

Title

AUTHOR: ....

GENRE: .... LENGTH: ....

PUBLISHER: .... YEAR PUBLISHED: ....

THEMES: ....

HOW I DISCOVERED THIS BOOK:

MEMORABLE QUOTES:

THOUGHTS & IMPRESSIONS:

BOOK NO.
....
15

◇ FICTION
◇ NONFICTION

DATE STARTED

DATE FINISHED

My Ratings

◇◇◇◇◇
ENJOYMENT

◇◇◇◇◇
CRAFT

◇◇◇◇◇
OVERALL

I'D RECOMMEND
THIS TO:

BOOK NO.

16

◇ FICTION
◇ NONFICTION

DATE STARTED

DATE FINISHED

My Ratings

◇◇◇◇◇
ENJOYMENT

◇◇◇◇◇
CRAFT

◇◇◇◇◇
OVERALL

I'D RECOMMEND
THIS TO:

Title

AUTHOR:
GENRE: LENGTH:
PUBLISHER: YEAR PUBLISHED:
THEMES:

HOW I DISCOVERED THIS BOOK:

MEMORABLE QUOTES:

THOUGHTS & IMPRESSIONS:

Title

AUTHOR: ....

GENRE: .... LENGTH: ....

PUBLISHER: .... YEAR PUBLISHED: ....

THEMES: ....

HOW I DISCOVERED THIS BOOK:

MEMORABLE QUOTES:

THOUGHTS & IMPRESSIONS:

◇ FICTION
◇ NONFICTION

DATE STARTED

DATE FINISHED

My Ratings

◇◇◇◇◇
ENJOYMENT

◇◇◇◇◇
CRAFT

◇◇◇◇◇
OVERALL

I'D RECOMMEND
THIS TO:

BOOK NO.

18

◇ FICTION
◇ NONFICTION

DATE STARTED

DATE FINISHED

My Ratings

◇◇◇◇◇
ENJOYMENT

◇◇◇◇◇
CRAFT

◇◇◇◇◇
OVERALL

I'D RECOMMEND
THIS TO:

Title

AUTHOR:

GENRE: LENGTH:

PUBLISHER: YEAR PUBLISHED:

THEMES:

HOW I DISCOVERED THIS BOOK:

MEMORABLE QUOTES:

THOUGHTS & IMPRESSIONS:

Title

AUTHOR: ....

GENRE: .... LENGTH: ....

PUBLISHER: .... YEAR PUBLISHED: ....

THEMES: ....

HOW I DISCOVERED THIS BOOK:

MEMORABLE QUOTES:

THOUGHTS & IMPRESSIONS:

◇ FICTION

◇ NONFICTION

DATE STARTED

DATE FINISHED

My Ratings

◇◇◇◇◇
ENJOYMENT

◇◇◇◇◇
CRAFT

◇◇◇◇◇
OVERALL

I'D RECOMMEND
THIS TO:

....
....
....
....

◇ FICTION
◇ NONFICTION

DATE STARTED

DATE FINISHED

My Ratings

◇◇◇◇◇
ENJOYMENT

◇◇◇◇◇
CRAFT

◇◇◇◇◇
OVERALL

I'D RECOMMEND
THIS TO:

Title

AUTHOR:

GENRE: LENGTH:

PUBLISHER: YEAR PUBLISHED:

THEMES:

HOW I DISCOVERED THIS BOOK:

MEMORABLE QUOTES:

THOUGHTS & IMPRESSIONS:

Title

AUTHOR: _____

GENRE: _____ LENGTH: _____

PUBLISHER: _____ YEAR PUBLISHED: ____

THEMES: _____

HOW I DISCOVERED THIS BOOK:

MEMORABLE QUOTES:

THOUGHTS & IMPRESSIONS:

◇ FICTION

◇ NONFICTION

DATE STARTED

DATE FINISHED

My Ratings

◇◇◇◇◇
ENJOYMENT

◇◇◇◇◇
CRAFT

◇◇◇◇◇
OVERALL

I'D RECOMMEND
THIS TO:

_____

_____

_____

_____

FIVE WAYS TO GET MORE OUT OF
YOUR READING LIFE

1. Identify your taste. We may all love to read, but that doesn't mean we love to read the same books. Readers with vibrant reading lives know what they like and why they like it. They know which section of the library holds joyful discoveries and which genre will satisfy the urge to settle in with a good book. When you pinpoint your taste, you can spend more time reading books you enjoy and less time with popular-but-wrong-for-you titles.

2. Build reading into your routine. Start each day with a chapter and a cup of coffee, or end the days with your novel and a cup of tea. Read a bit on your lunch break or while dinner cooks. When you establish a reading rhythm, you end up reading more. Not only do those small bursts of reading add up, they also provide bits of joy throughout the day.

3. Set the book aside. Life is too short to read books that aren't right for you—or that aren't right for you right now. When it comes to the reading life, timing is everything. If you feel stuck in your current read, don't be afraid to let it go. You can always come back to it later, or perhaps it simply isn't the right book for you. It took me years to realize there's nothing wrong with abandoning a book, and my reading life is now better for it. Life is too short to read books you aren't enjoying.

4. *Mix it up.* Bring some variety to your reading life by trying something new. If you tend to read new releases, try something old. If paperbacks are your go-to, try an audiobook while you water your plants or fold the laundry. If your staples are mysteries and thrillers, try a juicy family saga or breezy romance. While it's important to know your taste, it's also fun to explore a new corner of the library. At best, you find a new favorite author. At worst, you collect data that helps you find more books you love.

5. *Discuss and learn with fellow book lovers.* Digging into a book with fellow readers or the authors who wrote them helps you enjoy and appreciate your books even more. Check out the events page at your local bookstore or library. Gather a few discussion-loving friends to form a book club. If in-person options aren't available, find an author interview online or join a virtual book club. A bookish community, wherever you can find it, can provide rich reading experiences.

. . . .

It's always better to have too much to read than not enough.

≫——→ ANN PATCHETT ←——≪

BOOK NO.

22

◇ FICTION
◇ NONFICTION

DATE STARTED

DATE FINISHED

My Ratings

◇◇◇◇◇
ENJOYMENT

◇◇◇◇◇
CRAFT

◇◇◇◇◇
OVERALL

I'D RECOMMEND
THIS TO:

Title

AUTHOR:

GENRE: LENGTH:

PUBLISHER: YEAR PUBLISHED:

THEMES:

HOW I DISCOVERED THIS BOOK:

MEMORABLE QUOTES:

THOUGHTS & IMPRESSIONS:

Title

AUTHOR: ....

GENRE: .... LENGTH: ....

PUBLISHER: .... YEAR PUBLISHED: ....

THEMES: ....

HOW I DISCOVERED THIS BOOK:

MEMORABLE QUOTES:

THOUGHTS & IMPRESSIONS:

◇ FICTION
◇ NONFICTION

DATE STARTED

DATE FINISHED

My Ratings

◇◇◇◇◇
ENJOYMENT

◇◇◇◇◇
CRAFT

◇◇◇◇◇
OVERALL

I'D RECOMMEND
THIS TO:

....
....
....
....

BOOK NO.
....
24

◇ FICTION
◇ NONFICTION

DATE STARTED

DATE FINISHED

My Ratings

◇◇◇◇◇
ENJOYMENT

◇◇◇◇◇
CRAFT

◇◇◇◇◇
OVERALL

I'D RECOMMEND
THIS TO:

Title

AUTHOR:

GENRE: .... LENGTH: ....

PUBLISHER: .... YEAR PUBLISHED: ....

THEMES:

HOW I DISCOVERED THIS BOOK:

MEMORABLE QUOTES:

THOUGHTS & IMPRESSIONS:

Title

AUTHOR: ....

GENRE: .... LENGTH: ....

PUBLISHER: .... YEAR PUBLISHED: ....

THEMES: ....

HOW I DISCOVERED THIS BOOK:

MEMORABLE QUOTES:

THOUGHTS & IMPRESSIONS:

◇ FICTION

◇ NONFICTION

/ /

DATE STARTED

/ /

DATE FINISHED

My Ratings

◇◇◇◇◇

ENJOYMENT

◇◇◇◇◇

CRAFT

◇◇◇◇◇

OVERALL

I'D RECOMMEND
THIS TO:

.

....

....

....

....

BOOK NO.

26

◇ FICTION
◇ NONFICTION

DATE STARTED

DATE FINISHED

My Ratings

◇◇◇◇◇
ENJOYMENT

◇◇◇◇◇
CRAFT

◇◇◇◇◇
OVERALL

I'D RECOMMEND
THIS TO:

Title

AUTHOR:

GENRE: LENGTH:

PUBLISHER: YEAR PUBLISHED:

THEMES:

HOW I DISCOVERED THIS BOOK:

MEMORABLE QUOTES:

THOUGHTS & IMPRESSIONS:

Title

AUTHOR: ....

GENRE: .... LENGTH: ....

PUBLISHER: .... YEAR PUBLISHED: ....

THEMES: ....

HOW I DISCOVERED THIS BOOK:

MEMORABLE QUOTES:

THOUGHTS & IMPRESSIONS:

◇ FICTION

◇ NONFICTION

/ /

DATE STARTED

/ /

DATE FINISHED

My Ratings

◇◇◇◇◇
ENJOYMENT

◇◇◇◇◇
CRAFT

◇◇◇◇◇
OVERALL

I'D RECOMMEND
THIS TO:

....

....

....

....

BOOK NO.

28

◇ FICTION
◇ NONFICTION

DATE STARTED

DATE FINISHED

My Ratings

◇◇◇◇◇
ENJOYMENT

◇◇◇◇◇
CRAFT

◇◇◇◇◇
OVERALL

I'D RECOMMEND
THIS TO:

Title

AUTHOR:

GENRE: LENGTH:

PUBLISHER: YEAR PUBLISHED:

THEMES:

HOW I DISCOVERED THIS BOOK:

MEMORABLE QUOTES:

THOUGHTS & IMPRESSIONS:

Title

AUTHOR:

GENRE: LENGTH:

PUBLISHER: YEAR PUBLISHED:

THEMES:

HOW I DISCOVERED THIS BOOK:

MEMORABLE QUOTES:

THOUGHTS & IMPRESSIONS:

◇ FICTION
◇ NONFICTION

DATE STARTED

DATE FINISHED

My Ratings

◇◇◇◇◇
ENJOYMENT

◇◇◇◇◇
CRAFT

◇◇◇◇◇
OVERALL

I'D RECOMMEND
THIS TO:

BOOK NO.

30

◇ FICTION
◇ NONFICTION

DATE STARTED

DATE FINISHED

My Ratings

◇◇◇◇◇
ENJOYMENT

◇◇◇◇◇
CRAFT

◇◇◇◇◇
OVERALL

I'D RECOMMEND
THIS TO:

Title

AUTHOR:

GENRE: LENGTH:

PUBLISHER: YEAR PUBLISHED:

THEMES:

HOW I DISCOVERED THIS BOOK:

MEMORABLE QUOTES:

THOUGHTS & IMPRESSIONS:

Title

AUTHOR: ....

GENRE: .... LENGTH: ....

PUBLISHER: .... YEAR PUBLISHED: ....

THEMES: ....

HOW I DISCOVERED THIS BOOK:

MEMORABLE QUOTES:

THOUGHTS & IMPRESSIONS:

BOOK NO.
....
31

◇ FICTION
◇ NONFICTION

/ /
DATE STARTED

/ /
DATE FINISHED

My Ratings

◇◇◇◇◇
ENJOYMENT

◇◇◇◇◇
CRAFT

◇◇◇◇◇
OVERALL

I'D RECOMMEND
THIS TO:

....
....
....
....

BOOK NO.

32

◇ FICTION
◇ NONFICTION

DATE STARTED

DATE FINISHED

My Ratings

◇◇◇◇◇
ENJOYMENT

◇◇◇◇◇
CRAFT

◇◇◇◇◇
OVERALL

I'D RECOMMEND
THIS TO:

Title

AUTHOR:

GENRE: LENGTH:

PUBLISHER: YEAR PUBLISHED:

THEMES:

HOW I DISCOVERED THIS BOOK:

MEMORABLE QUOTES:

THOUGHTS & IMPRESSIONS:

Title

AUTHOR:

GENRE: .... LENGTH: ....

PUBLISHER: .... YEAR PUBLISHED: ....

THEMES: ....

HOW I DISCOVERED THIS BOOK:

MEMORABLE QUOTES:

THOUGHTS & IMPRESSIONS:

◇ FICTION

◇ NONFICTION

DATE STARTED

DATE FINISHED

My Ratings

◇◇◇◇◇
ENJOYMENT

◇◇◇◇◇
CRAFT

◇◇◇◇◇
OVERALL

I'D RECOMMEND
THIS TO:

BOOK NO.

34

◇ FICTION
◇ NONFICTION

| / / |

DATE STARTED

| / / |

DATE FINISHED

My Ratings

◇◇◇◇◇
ENJOYMENT

◇◇◇◇◇
CRAFT

◇◇◇◇◇
OVERALL

I'D RECOMMEND
THIS TO:

....

....

....

....

Title

AUTHOR: ....

GENRE: .... LENGTH: ....

PUBLISHER: .... YEAR PUBLISHED: ....

THEMES: ....

HOW I DISCOVERED THIS BOOK:

MEMORABLE QUOTES:

THOUGHTS & IMPRESSIONS:

Title

AUTHOR: ....

GENRE: .... LENGTH: ....

PUBLISHER: .... YEAR PUBLISHED: ....

THEMES: ....

◇ FICTION

◇ NONFICTION

DATE STARTED

DATE FINISHED

HOW I DISCOVERED THIS BOOK:

MEMORABLE QUOTES:

THOUGHTS & IMPRESSIONS:

My Ratings

◇◇◇◇◇
ENJOYMENT

◇◇◇◇◇
CRAFT

◇◇◇◇◇
OVERALL

I'D RECOMMEND
THIS TO:

....
....
....
....

BOOK NO.

36

◇ FICTION
◇ NONFICTION

DATE STARTED

DATE FINISHED

My Ratings

◇◇◇◇◇
ENJOYMENT

◇◇◇◇◇
CRAFT

◇◇◇◇◇
OVERALL

I'D RECOMMEND
THIS TO:

Title

AUTHOR:

GENRE: LENGTH:

PUBLISHER: YEAR PUBLISHED:

THEMES:

HOW I DISCOVERED THIS BOOK:

MEMORABLE QUOTES:

THOUGHTS & IMPRESSIONS:

Title

AUTHOR: ....

GENRE: .... LENGTH: ....

PUBLISHER: .... YEAR PUBLISHED: ....

THEMES: ....

◇ FICTION
◇ NONFICTION

HOW I DISCOVERED THIS BOOK:

MEMORABLE QUOTES:

THOUGHTS & IMPRESSIONS:

DATE STARTED

DATE FINISHED

My Ratings

◇◇◇◇◇
ENJOYMENT

◇◇◇◇◇
CRAFT

◇◇◇◇◇
OVERALL

I'D RECOMMEND
THIS TO:

....
....
....
....

BOOK NO.
....
38

◇ FICTION
◇ NONFICTION

DATE STARTED

DATE FINISHED

My Ratings

◇◇◇◇◇
ENJOYMENT

◇◇◇◇◇
CRAFT

◇◇◇◇◇
OVERALL

I'D RECOMMEND
THIS TO:

Title

AUTHOR:

GENRE: LENGTH:

PUBLISHER: YEAR PUBLISHED:

THEMES:

HOW I DISCOVERED THIS BOOK:

MEMORABLE QUOTES:

THOUGHTS & IMPRESSIONS:

Title

AUTHOR: ....

GENRE: .... LENGTH: ....

PUBLISHER: .... YEAR PUBLISHED: ....

THEMES: ....

HOW I DISCOVERED THIS BOOK:

MEMORABLE QUOTES:

THOUGHTS & IMPRESSIONS:

◇ FICTION

◇ NONFICTION

/ /

DATE STARTED

/ /

DATE FINISHED

My Ratings

◇◇◇◇◇
ENJOYMENT

◇◇◇◇◇
CRAFT

◇◇◇◇◇
OVERALL

I'D RECOMMEND
THIS TO:

....

....

....

....

BOOK NO.

....

40

◇ FICTION
◇ NONFICTION

DATE STARTED

DATE FINISHED

My Ratings

◇◇◇◇◇
ENJOYMENT

◇◇◇◇◇
CRAFT

◇◇◇◇◇
OVERALL

I'D RECOMMEND
THIS TO:

Title

AUTHOR:

GENRE: LENGTH:

PUBLISHER: YEAR PUBLISHED:

THEMES:

HOW I DISCOVERED THIS BOOK:

MEMORABLE QUOTES:

THOUGHTS & IMPRESSIONS:

Title

AUTHOR: ....

GENRE: .... LENGTH: ....

PUBLISHER: .... YEAR PUBLISHED: ....

THEMES: ....

HOW I DISCOVERED THIS BOOK:

MEMORABLE QUOTES:

THOUGHTS & IMPRESSIONS:

◇ FICTION

◇ NONFICTION

DATE STARTED

DATE FINISHED

My Ratings

◇◇◇◇◇
ENJOYMENT

◇◇◇◇◇
CRAFT

◇◇◇◇◇
OVERALL

I'D RECOMMEND
THIS TO:

- FIVE TIPS TO HELP YOU READ MORE -

When it comes to reading, quality is far more important than quantity. And yet, with so many good books to choose from, many readers want to enjoy more of them. Try these strategies if you would like to finish more books this year.

1. Keep a "to be read" list. Deciding what to read next takes up precious reading time. Keep a list of all the books you want to read for easy reference, and skip the stress of searching.

2. Surround yourself with good books. Many people prioritize reading time if, and only if, they're excited about what they're reading right now. So make sure you're never at a loss for something good to read! Try placing a few titles you're excited about on your nightstand or coffee table where they're easy to reach for. Next time you go to the library, check out multiple books in one trip so you have a few extra on hand. That way, when you finish one book, you always have another at the ready.

3. Read multiple books at once. Experiment with having one nonfiction book, one novel, and one audiobook in rotation at any given time so you're more likely to have the right book for the moment—and your mood.

4. Seize the spare minutes. Keep a book in the car or downloaded on your phone and sneak in a few pages while waiting for the coffee to brew, while standing in line at the grocery store, or between errands. Those small bursts of reading add up.

5. Plan a reading marathon. We're all familiar with the pleasure of a good movie marathon. Try the same with books. Set aside a day to sit in your comfy reading spot, grab a beverage and some snacks, and get lost in a good story.

I could spend the rest of my life reading,
just satisfying my curiosity.

⇛ —→ ⇒ MALCOLM X ⇐ ←— ⇚

BOOK NO.

42

◇ FICTION
◇ NONFICTION

DATE STARTED

DATE FINISHED

My Ratings

◇◇◇◇◇
ENJOYMENT

◇◇◇◇◇
CRAFT

◇◇◇◇◇
OVERALL

I'D RECOMMEND
THIS TO:

Title

AUTHOR:

GENRE: LENGTH:

PUBLISHER: YEAR PUBLISHED:

THEMES:

HOW I DISCOVERED THIS BOOK:

MEMORABLE QUOTES:

THOUGHTS & IMPRESSIONS:

Title

AUTHOR: ....

GENRE: .... LENGTH: ....

PUBLISHER: .... YEAR PUBLISHED: ....

THEMES: ....

◇ FICTION

◇ NONFICTION

```
       /   /
```
DATE STARTED

```
       /   /
```
DATE FINISHED

HOW I DISCOVERED THIS BOOK:

MEMORABLE QUOTES:

THOUGHTS & IMPRESSIONS:

My Ratings

◇◇◇◇◇
ENJOYMENT

◇◇◇◇◇
CRAFT

◇◇◇◇◇
OVERALL

I'D RECOMMEND
THIS TO:

....

....

....

....

BOOK NO.
. . . .
44

◇ FICTION
◇ NONFICTION

DATE STARTED

DATE FINISHED

My Ratings

◇◇◇◇◇
ENJOYMENT

◇◇◇◇◇
CRAFT

◇◇◇◇◇
OVERALL

I'D RECOMMEND
THIS TO:

Title

AUTHOR: ....

GENRE: .... LENGTH: ....

PUBLISHER: .... YEAR PUBLISHED: ....

THEMES: ....

HOW I DISCOVERED THIS BOOK:

MEMORABLE QUOTES:

THOUGHTS & IMPRESSIONS:

Title

AUTHOR: ....

GENRE: .... LENGTH: ....

PUBLISHER: .... YEAR PUBLISHED: ....

THEMES: ....

◇ FICTION

◇ NONFICTION

| / | / |

DATE STARTED

| / | / |

DATE FINISHED

HOW I DISCOVERED THIS BOOK:

MEMORABLE QUOTES:

THOUGHTS & IMPRESSIONS:

My Ratings

◇◇◇◇◇
ENJOYMENT

◇◇◇◇◇
CRAFT

◇◇◇◇◇
OVERALL

I'D RECOMMEND
THIS TO:

....
....
....
....

BOOK NO.
46

◇ FICTION
◇ NONFICTION

DATE STARTED

DATE FINISHED

My Ratings

◇◇◇◇◇
ENJOYMENT

◇◇◇◇◇
CRAFT

◇◇◇◇◇
OVERALL

I'D RECOMMEND
THIS TO:

Title

AUTHOR:

GENRE: LENGTH:

PUBLISHER: YEAR PUBLISHED:

THEMES:

HOW I DISCOVERED THIS BOOK:

MEMORABLE QUOTES:

THOUGHTS & IMPRESSIONS:

Books have to
be *heavy* because
the whole *world's*
inside them.

— *Cornelia Funke*

BOOK NO.
47

◇ FICTION
◇ NONFICTION

/ /
DATE STARTED

/ /
DATE FINISHED

My Ratings

◇◇◇◇◇
ENJOYMENT

◇◇◇◇◇
CRAFT

◇◇◇◇◇
OVERALL

I'D RECOMMEND
THIS TO:

Title

AUTHOR:

GENRE: LENGTH:

PUBLISHER: YEAR PUBLISHED:

THEMES:

HOW I DISCOVERED THIS BOOK:

MEMORABLE QUOTES:

THOUGHTS & IMPRESSIONS:

Title

AUTHOR:

GENRE: _____ LENGTH: _____

PUBLISHER: _____ YEAR PUBLISHED: _____

THEMES:

◇ FICTION

◇ NONFICTION

DATE STARTED

DATE FINISHED

HOW I DISCOVERED THIS BOOK:

MEMORABLE QUOTES:

My Ratings

◇◇◇◇◇
ENJOYMENT

◇◇◇◇◇
CRAFT

THOUGHTS & IMPRESSIONS:

◇◇◇◇◇
OVERALL

I'D RECOMMEND
THIS TO:

BOOK NO.
....
49

◇ FICTION
◇ NONFICTION

DATE STARTED

DATE FINISHED

My Ratings

◇◇◇◇◇
ENJOYMENT

◇◇◇◇◇
CRAFT

◇◇◇◇◇
OVERALL

I'D RECOMMEND
THIS TO:

Title

AUTHOR:

GENRE: LENGTH:

PUBLISHER: YEAR PUBLISHED:

THEMES:

HOW I DISCOVERED THIS BOOK:

MEMORABLE QUOTES:

THOUGHTS & IMPRESSIONS:

Title

AUTHOR: ....

GENRE: .... LENGTH: ....

PUBLISHER: .... YEAR PUBLISHED: ....

THEMES: ....

HOW I DISCOVERED THIS BOOK:

MEMORABLE QUOTES:

THOUGHTS & IMPRESSIONS:

◇ FICTION

◇ NONFICTION

/ /

DATE STARTED

/ /

DATE FINISHED

My Ratings

◇◇◇◇◇
ENJOYMENT

◇◇◇◇◇
CRAFT

◇◇◇◇◇
OVERALL

I'D RECOMMEND
THIS TO:

....
....
....
....

BOOK NO.

51

◇ FICTION
◇ NONFICTION

DATE STARTED

DATE FINISHED

My Ratings

◇◇◇◇◇
ENJOYMENT

◇◇◇◇◇
CRAFT

◇◇◇◇◇
OVERALL

I'D RECOMMEND
THIS TO:

Title

AUTHOR:

GENRE: LENGTH:

PUBLISHER: YEAR PUBLISHED:

THEMES:

HOW I DISCOVERED THIS BOOK:

MEMORABLE QUOTES:

THOUGHTS & IMPRESSIONS:

Title

AUTHOR:

GENRE: LENGTH:

PUBLISHER: YEAR PUBLISHED:

THEMES:

◇ FICTION

◇ NONFICTION

DATE STARTED

DATE FINISHED

HOW I DISCOVERED THIS BOOK:

MEMORABLE QUOTES:

THOUGHTS & IMPRESSIONS:

My Ratings

◇◇◇◇◇
ENJOYMENT

◇◇◇◇◇
CRAFT

◇◇◇◇◇
OVERALL

I'D RECOMMEND
THIS TO:

BOOK NO.

53

◇ FICTION

◇ NONFICTION

DATE STARTED

DATE FINISHED

My Ratings

◇◇◇◇◇
ENJOYMENT

◇◇◇◇◇
CRAFT

◇◇◇◇◇
OVERALL

I'D RECOMMEND
THIS TO:

Title

AUTHOR:

GENRE: .... LENGTH:

PUBLISHER: .... YEAR PUBLISHED:

THEMES:

HOW I DISCOVERED THIS BOOK:

MEMORABLE QUOTES:

THOUGHTS & IMPRESSIONS:

Title

AUTHOR: ....

GENRE: .... LENGTH: ....

PUBLISHER: .... YEAR PUBLISHED: ....

THEMES: ....

◇ FICTION

◇ NONFICTION

HOW I DISCOVERED THIS BOOK:

DATE STARTED

DATE FINISHED

MEMORABLE QUOTES:

My Ratings

◇◇◇◇◇
ENJOYMENT

◇◇◇◇◇
CRAFT

THOUGHTS & IMPRESSIONS:

◇◇◇◇◇
OVERALL

I'D RECOMMEND
THIS TO:

- TIPS FOR OVERCOMING A READING RUT -

I'd like to think it happens to all readers, because it certainly happens to me: the dreaded reading rut, where I find myself reading the same kind of book over and over again—and not in a good way. Or when, despite the hundreds of titles on my "to be read" list, not a single one sounds appealing right now. I'm in a rut, and I need help getting myself out of it.

Over the years, I've collected advice from fellow readers to help me overcome the occasional reading rut. Next time your reading life feels a little tired, try this broad-strokes, systematic approach to find a new groove:

Read something different. Next time you visit the library, try to choose books from several different categories. For example, you could pick up one nonfiction, one fiction, one graphic novel, and one essay collection. Then, when you find yourself stuck in a rut, change it up by selecting something completely different from your current read.

Read something short. Sometimes when I'm in a rut, I don't feel like reading anything at all. To gain momentum, I pick up a short book—something I can read in one day or one sitting. It makes me feel accomplished, helps me reach a small goal, and propels me into my next great read.

Reread one of your favorites. Instead of spinning your wheels deciding what to read next, go back to a book you know you'll love. Revisit a childhood classic and experience the magic of being wrapped up in a familiar story. Reread an all-time favorite book and highlight the best lines. (You should see my copy of *Pride and Prejudice*!) Reacquaint yourself with beloved characters and note how they have influenced your own life.

Try something new. This is the best time to take a risk. You have nothing to lose by trying something new when you're in a reading rut. Ask a trusted friend for a recommendation in a genre you typically avoid. Attempt a new-to-you format, such as an audiobook or graphic memoir. Instead of reading in bed each night, try reading at the kitchen counter for a few minutes in the morning. A dose of spontaneity might be just the thing to reinvigorate your reading life.

• •

I've never known any trouble that an
hour's reading didn't assuage.

⇒——→ ARTHUR SCHOPENHAUER ←——⇐

BOOK NO.

55

◇ FICTION
◇ NONFICTION

DATE STARTED

DATE FINISHED

My Ratings

◇◇◇◇◇
ENJOYMENT

◇◇◇◇◇
CRAFT

◇◇◇◇◇
OVERALL

I'D RECOMMEND
THIS TO:

Title

AUTHOR:

GENRE: LENGTH:

PUBLISHER: YEAR PUBLISHED:

THEMES:

HOW I DISCOVERED THIS BOOK:

MEMORABLE QUOTES:

THOUGHTS & IMPRESSIONS:

Title

AUTHOR:

GENRE: LENGTH:

PUBLISHER: YEAR PUBLISHED:

THEMES:

HOW I DISCOVERED THIS BOOK:

MEMORABLE QUOTES:

THOUGHTS & IMPRESSIONS:

◇ FICTION
◇ NONFICTION

DATE STARTED

DATE FINISHED

My Ratings

◇◇◇◇◇
ENJOYMENT

◇◇◇◇◇
CRAFT

◇◇◇◇◇
OVERALL

I'D RECOMMEND
THIS TO:

BOOK NO.
....
57

◇ FICTION
◇ NONFICTION

DATE STARTED

DATE FINISHED

My Ratings

◇◇◇◇◇
ENJOYMENT

◇◇◇◇◇
CRAFT

◇◇◇◇◇
OVERALL

I'D RECOMMEND
THIS TO:

Title

AUTHOR:
GENRE: LENGTH:
PUBLISHER: YEAR PUBLISHED:
THEMES:

HOW I DISCOVERED THIS BOOK:

MEMORABLE QUOTES:

THOUGHTS & IMPRESSIONS:

Title

AUTHOR: _____

GENRE: _____ LENGTH: _____

PUBLISHER: _____ YEAR PUBLISHED: _____

THEMES: _____

HOW I DISCOVERED THIS BOOK:

MEMORABLE QUOTES:

THOUGHTS & IMPRESSIONS:

◇ FICTION

◇ NONFICTION

_ _ / _ _ / _ _

DATE STARTED

_ _ / _ _ / _ _

DATE FINISHED

My Ratings

◇◇◇◇◇
ENJOYMENT

◇◇◇◇◇
CRAFT

◇◇◇◇◇
OVERALL

I'D RECOMMEND
THIS TO:

_____

_____

_____

BOOK NO.
....
59

◇ FICTION
◇ NONFICTION

| / / |
| DATE STARTED |

| / / |
| DATE FINISHED |

My Ratings

◇◇◇◇◇
ENJOYMENT

◇◇◇◇◇
CRAFT

◇◇◇◇◇
OVERALL

I'D RECOMMEND
THIS TO:

_____
_____
_____

Title

AUTHOR: _____

GENRE: _____ LENGTH: _____

PUBLISHER: _____ YEAR PUBLISHED: _____

THEMES: _____

HOW I DISCOVERED THIS BOOK:

MEMORABLE QUOTES:

THOUGHTS & IMPRESSIONS:

Title

AUTHOR: ....

GENRE: .... LENGTH: ....

PUBLISHER: .... YEAR PUBLISHED: ....

THEMES: ....

HOW I DISCOVERED THIS BOOK:

MEMORABLE QUOTES:

THOUGHTS & IMPRESSIONS:

◇ FICTION

◇ NONFICTION

◻ / /
DATE STARTED

◻ / /
DATE FINISHED

My Ratings

◇◇◇◇◇
ENJOYMENT

◇◇◇◇◇
CRAFT

◇◇◇◇◇
OVERALL

I'D RECOMMEND
THIS TO:

....
....
....
....

BOOK NO.
. . . .
61

◇ FICTION
◇ NONFICTION

DATE STARTED

DATE FINISHED

My Ratings

◇◇◇◇◇
ENJOYMENT

◇◇◇◇◇
CRAFT

◇◇◇◇◇
OVERALL

I'D RECOMMEND
THIS TO:

Title

AUTHOR:
GENRE: LENGTH:
PUBLISHER: YEAR PUBLISHED:
THEMES:

HOW I DISCOVERED THIS BOOK:

MEMORABLE QUOTES:

THOUGHTS & IMPRESSIONS:

Title

AUTHOR:

GENRE: LENGTH:

PUBLISHER: YEAR PUBLISHED:

THEMES:

HOW I DISCOVERED THIS BOOK:

MEMORABLE QUOTES:

THOUGHTS & IMPRESSIONS:

◇ FICTION

◇ NONFICTION

/ /

DATE STARTED

/ /

DATE FINISHED

My Ratings

◇◇◇◇◇
ENJOYMENT

◇◇◇◇◇
CRAFT

◇◇◇◇◇
OVERALL

I'D RECOMMEND
THIS TO:

- A BOOK CLUB GUIDE -

Forming and Sustaining an Engaging Discussion Group

Book clubs provide bookish conversation, community, account-ability, and ideas for what to read next. Here are some tips for getting the most from your book club.

Forming a Group. Email a broad list of friends to gauge interest or solicit acquaintances from a group of coworkers, school parents, or a fitness class. If you'd prefer to join an existing group, many libraries, bookstores, and community centers run their own book clubs. Five to ten members seems to be the magic size, but if you can't gather that many, don't despair! Many successful groups begin with two friends talking books over coffee and gradually add members over time. With plenty of bookish conversations and a good helping of snacks, your book club members might become your closest friends—even if you started as strangers.

Deciding What to Read. There is no wrong way to choose what to read next. Perhaps one of these options will feel right for your group:

1. *Stick with a forever theme:* contemporary fiction or classics, mysteries or romance, prize winners or middle grade books.
2. *Choose one theme for the year:* book to movie adaptations, books in translation, graphic novels.
3. *Take turns choosing books, no questions asked.*

4. *Nominate a group leader to narrow down the selection to three titles, and then vote.*

5. *Gather as a literary society:* Instead of reading and discussing the same book, every member shares whatever they happen to be reading at the moment.

Planning When and Where to Meet. Whether you choose to meet weekly, monthly, or quarterly, a regular meeting time is essential. Some book clubs meet at members' homes, rotating hosting duties. Some groups meet at a local coffee shop or restaurant. A small group can even meet at the park and walk laps while discussing their book. Food is a big part of many book club plans, and there's nothing wrong with that! If you'd like to enjoy food and drink together, decide on whether to host potluck-style dinners, share snacks for nibbling, or order takeout to save time.

Sparking Great Conversations. A great discussion starts with the right book: you want a selection that gets readers talking! Books with ambiguous endings, interesting narrative structures, or unreliable narrators are likely to spark great conversations.

Many book clubs designate a leader to guide the conversation for each meeting. Some clubs rotate; some draw a name out of a hat for each meeting. This "book boss" is in charge of transitioning the club from socializing to serious discussion, asking the opening questions, steering the conversation back when it veers off track, and making sure no one dominates the conversation. To keep the conversation going, try this simple phrase: "Say more about that." This leads to deeper discussions and requires members to think carefully about their opinions.

TEN QUESTIONS THAT WORK
FOR ANY BOOK DISCUSSION

1. What was your initial reaction to the book? How did that evolve as you continued to read?

2. What do you think the title means? Did your understanding of the title change as you read the story? Can you think of a title that's more suitable?

3. Did the characters seem real to you? Did you find their thoughts and actions to be believable or relatable? How did they grow and change throughout the course of the story?

4. What was your favorite scene? Favorite quote?

5. What specific themes stood out to you? What message do you think the author was trying to get across to the reader?

6. Could the book have taken place anywhere, or was the setting crucial to the story?

7. Did the story change the way you think about an event, place, or time?

8. How did the author structure the book? For example, was the structure based on the timeline, viewpoints, dialogue, or language? How did this affect the story?

9. How did you feel about the ending? Did the resolution of the book feel right to you?

10. Did the book change your mind about anything? Give you a new perspective? Prompt you to think about a person or a topic in a new way?

WONDERFULLY DISCUSSABLE BOOKS

For a memorable book club discussion, you need a book that gets readers talking! These thought-provoking titles will fuel hours of bookish conversation.

◇ *The Light Between Oceans* | M.L. Stedman

◇ *The Red Tent* | Anita Diamant

◇ *Behold the Dreamers* | Imbolo Mbue

◇ *Olive Kitteridge* | Elizabeth Strout

◇ *Five-Carat Soul* | James McBride

◇ *Tell the Wolves I'm Home* | Carol Rifka Brunt

◇ *When Breath Becomes Air* | Paul Kalanithi

◇ *Hannah Coulter* | Wendell Berry

◇ *The Pearl That Broke Its Shell* | Nadia Hashimi

◇ *Everyone Brave Is Forgiven* | Chris Cleave

◇ *We Were the Lucky Ones* | Georgia Hunter

◇ *So You've Been Publicly Shamed* | Jon Ronson

◇ *Interpreter of Maladies* | Jhumpa Lahiri

◇ *I Let You Go* | Clare Mackintosh

◇ *Year of Wonders* | Geraldine Brooks

◇ *The Nickel Boys* | Colson Whitehead

◇ *Tenth of December* | George Saunders

◇ *Before We Visit the Goddess* | Chitra Banerjee Divakaruni

◇ *The Road* | Cormac McCarthy

◇ *An American Marriage* | Tayari Jones

BOOK NO.

63

◇ FICTION
◇ NONFICTION

DATE STARTED

DATE FINISHED

My Ratings

◇◇◇◇◇
ENJOYMENT

◇◇◇◇◇
CRAFT

◇◇◇◇◇
OVERALL

I'D RECOMMEND
THIS TO:

Title

AUTHOR:

GENRE: LENGTH:

PUBLISHER: YEAR PUBLISHED:

THEMES:

HOW I DISCOVERED THIS BOOK:

MEMORABLE QUOTES:

THOUGHTS & IMPRESSIONS:

Title

AUTHOR: ....

GENRE: .... LENGTH: ....

PUBLISHER: .... YEAR PUBLISHED: ....

THEMES: ....

HOW I DISCOVERED THIS BOOK:

MEMORABLE QUOTES:

THOUGHTS & IMPRESSIONS:

BOOK NO.

64

◇ FICTION

◇ NONFICTION

DATE STARTED

DATE FINISHED

My Ratings

◇◇◇◇◇
ENJOYMENT

◇◇◇◇◇
CRAFT

◇◇◇◇◇
OVERALL

I'D RECOMMEND
THIS TO:

◇ FICTION

◇ NONFICTION

DATE STARTED

DATE FINISHED

My Ratings

◇◇◇◇◇
ENJOYMENT

◇◇◇◇◇
CRAFT

◇◇◇◇◇
OVERALL

I'D RECOMMEND
THIS TO:

Title

AUTHOR:

GENRE: .... LENGTH:

PUBLISHER: .... YEAR PUBLISHED:

THEMES:

HOW I DISCOVERED THIS BOOK:

MEMORABLE QUOTES:

THOUGHTS & IMPRESSIONS:

Title

AUTHOR: _____

GENRE: _____ LENGTH: _____

PUBLISHER: _____ YEAR PUBLISHED: _____

THEMES: _____

◇ FICTION

◇ NONFICTION

/   /

DATE STARTED

/   /

DATE FINISHED

HOW I DISCOVERED THIS BOOK:

MEMORABLE QUOTES:

My Ratings

◇◇◇◇◇
ENJOYMENT

◇◇◇◇◇
CRAFT

THOUGHTS & IMPRESSIONS:

◇◇◇◇◇
OVERALL

I'D RECOMMEND
THIS TO:

_____

_____

_____

She read books
as one would
breathe air,
to fill up and
live.

—Annie Dillard

Title

AUTHOR: ....
GENRE: .... LENGTH: ....
PUBLISHER: .... YEAR PUBLISHED: ....
THEMES: ....

HOW I DISCOVERED THIS BOOK:

MEMORABLE QUOTES:

THOUGHTS & IMPRESSIONS:

◇ FICTION
◇ NONFICTION

/ /
DATE STARTED

/ /
DATE FINISHED

My Ratings

◇◇◇◇◇
ENJOYMENT

◇◇◇◇◇
CRAFT

◇◇◇◇◇
OVERALL

I'D RECOMMEND
THIS TO:

....
....
....

BOOK NO.
68

◇ FICTION
◇ NONFICTION

DATE STARTED

DATE FINISHED

My Ratings

◇◇◇◇◇
ENJOYMENT

◇◇◇◇◇
CRAFT

◇◇◇◇◇
OVERALL

I'D RECOMMEND
THIS TO:

Title

AUTHOR:

GENRE: LENGTH:

PUBLISHER: YEAR PUBLISHED:

THEMES:

HOW I DISCOVERED THIS BOOK:

MEMORABLE QUOTES:

THOUGHTS & IMPRESSIONS:

Title

AUTHOR: ....

GENRE: .... LENGTH: ....

PUBLISHER: .... YEAR PUBLISHED: ....

THEMES: ....

HOW I DISCOVERED THIS BOOK:

MEMORABLE QUOTES:

THOUGHTS & IMPRESSIONS:

◇ FICTION

◇ NONFICTION

┌──────────────────┐
│   /   /   │
└──────────────────┘
DATE STARTED

┌──────────────────┐
│   /   /   │
└──────────────────┘
DATE FINISHED

My Ratings

◇◇◇◇◇
ENJOYMENT

◇◇◇◇◇
CRAFT

◇◇◇◇◇
OVERALL

I'D RECOMMEND
THIS TO:

....

....

....

....

BOOK NO.

70

◇ FICTION
◇ NONFICTION

DATE STARTED

DATE FINISHED

My Ratings

◇◇◇◇◇
ENJOYMENT

◇◇◇◇◇
CRAFT

◇◇◇◇◇
OVERALL

I'D RECOMMEND
THIS TO:

Title

AUTHOR:

GENRE: LENGTH:

PUBLISHER: YEAR PUBLISHED:

THEMES:

HOW I DISCOVERED THIS BOOK:

MEMORABLE QUOTES:

THOUGHTS & IMPRESSIONS:

Title

AUTHOR: _____

GENRE: _____ LENGTH: _____

PUBLISHER: _____ YEAR PUBLISHED: _____

THEMES: _____

HOW I DISCOVERED THIS BOOK:

MEMORABLE QUOTES:

THOUGHTS & IMPRESSIONS:

◇ FICTION

◇ NONFICTION

_____
/ /
DATE STARTED

_____
/ /
DATE FINISHED

My Ratings

◇◇◇◇◇
ENJOYMENT

◇◇◇◇◇
CRAFT

◇◇◇◇◇
OVERALL

I'D RECOMMEND
THIS TO:

_____
_____
_____
_____

BOOK NO.

....

72

◇ FICTION
◇ NONFICTION

DATE STARTED

DATE FINISHED

My Ratings

◇◇◇◇◇
ENJOYMENT

◇◇◇◇◇
CRAFT

◇◇◇◇◇
OVERALL

I'D RECOMMEND
THIS TO:

....

....

....

....

Title

AUTHOR:

GENRE: LENGTH:

PUBLISHER: YEAR PUBLISHED:

THEMES:

HOW I DISCOVERED THIS BOOK:

MEMORABLE QUOTES:

THOUGHTS & IMPRESSIONS:

Title

AUTHOR:

GENRE: _____ LENGTH: _____

PUBLISHER: _____ YEAR PUBLISHED: _____

THEMES: _____

HOW I DISCOVERED THIS BOOK:

MEMORABLE QUOTES:

THOUGHTS & IMPRESSIONS:

◇ FICTION

◇ NONFICTION

DATE STARTED

DATE FINISHED

My Ratings

◇◇◇◇◇
ENJOYMENT

◇◇◇◇◇
CRAFT

◇◇◇◇◇
OVERALL

I'D RECOMMEND
THIS TO:

BOOK NO.
74

◇ FICTION
◇ NONFICTION

⬚ / /
DATE STARTED

⬚ / /
DATE FINISHED

My Ratings

◇◇◇◇◇
ENJOYMENT

◇◇◇◇◇
CRAFT

◇◇◇◇◇
OVERALL

I'D RECOMMEND
THIS TO:

_____
_____
_____

Title

AUTHOR: _____

GENRE: _____ LENGTH: _____

PUBLISHER: _____ YEAR PUBLISHED: _____

THEMES: _____

HOW I DISCOVERED THIS BOOK:

MEMORABLE QUOTES:

THOUGHTS & IMPRESSIONS:

Title

AUTHOR:

GENRE: .... LENGTH:

PUBLISHER: .... YEAR PUBLISHED:

THEMES:

HOW I DISCOVERED THIS BOOK:

MEMORABLE QUOTES:

THOUGHTS & IMPRESSIONS:

◇ FICTION

◇ NONFICTION

DATE STARTED

DATE FINISHED

My Ratings

◇◇◇◇◇
ENJOYMENT

◇◇◇◇◇
CRAFT

◇◇◇◇◇
OVERALL

I'D RECOMMEND
THIS TO:

BOOK NO.

76

◇ FICTION
◇ NONFICTION

DATE STARTED

DATE FINISHED

My Ratings

◇◇◇◇◇
ENJOYMENT

◇◇◇◇◇
CRAFT

◇◇◇◇◇
OVERALL

I'D RECOMMEND
THIS TO:

Title

AUTHOR:

GENRE: LENGTH:

PUBLISHER: YEAR PUBLISHED:

THEMES:

HOW I DISCOVERED THIS BOOK:

MEMORABLE QUOTES:

THOUGHTS & IMPRESSIONS:

Title

AUTHOR:

GENRE: LENGTH:

PUBLISHER: YEAR PUBLISHED:

THEMES:

HOW I DISCOVERED THIS BOOK:

MEMORABLE QUOTES:

THOUGHTS & IMPRESSIONS:

◇ FICTION

◇ NONFICTION

```
/    /
```
DATE STARTED

```
/    /
```
DATE FINISHED

My Ratings

◇◇◇◇◇
ENJOYMENT

◇◇◇◇◇
CRAFT

◇◇◇◇◇
OVERALL

I'D RECOMMEND
THIS TO:

BOOK NO.

78

◇ FICTION
◇ NONFICTION

_____
/   /
DATE STARTED

_____
/   /
DATE FINISHED

My Ratings

◇◇◇◇◇
ENJOYMENT

◇◇◇◇◇
CRAFT

◇◇◇◇◇
OVERALL

I'D RECOMMEND
THIS TO:

_____

_____

_____

_____

Title

AUTHOR:

GENRE: LENGTH:

PUBLISHER: YEAR PUBLISHED:

THEMES:

HOW I DISCOVERED THIS BOOK:

MEMORABLE QUOTES:

THOUGHTS & IMPRESSIONS:

Title

AUTHOR: _____

GENRE: _____ LENGTH: _____

PUBLISHER: _____ YEAR PUBLISHED: _____

THEMES: _____

HOW I DISCOVERED THIS BOOK:

MEMORABLE QUOTES:

THOUGHTS & IMPRESSIONS:

◇ FICTION

◇ NONFICTION

| / | / |

DATE STARTED

| / | / |

DATE FINISHED

My Ratings

◇◇◇◇◇
ENJOYMENT

◇◇◇◇◇
CRAFT

◇◇◇◇◇
OVERALL

I'D RECOMMEND
THIS TO:

_____

_____

_____

_____

BOOK NO.
80

◇ FICTION
◇ NONFICTION

DATE STARTED

DATE FINISHED

My Ratings

◇◇◇◇◇
ENJOYMENT

◇◇◇◇◇
CRAFT

◇◇◇◇◇
OVERALL

I'D RECOMMEND
THIS TO:

Title

AUTHOR:

GENRE: _____ LENGTH:

PUBLISHER: _____ YEAR PUBLISHED:

THEMES:

HOW I DISCOVERED THIS BOOK:

MEMORABLE QUOTES:

THOUGHTS & IMPRESSIONS:

Title

AUTHOR: _____

GENRE: _____ LENGTH: _____

PUBLISHER: _____ YEAR PUBLISHED: _____

THEMES: _____

HOW I DISCOVERED THIS BOOK:

MEMORABLE QUOTES:

THOUGHTS & IMPRESSIONS:

◇ FICTION

◇ NONFICTION

/ /

DATE STARTED

/ /

DATE FINISHED

My Ratings

◇◇◇◇◇

ENJOYMENT

◇◇◇◇◇

CRAFT

◇◇◇◇◇

OVERALL

I'D RECOMMEND
THIS TO:

_____
_____
_____
_____

- TOOLS FOR THE READING LIFE -

1. *Your reading journal* — for approaching your reading life with intention

2. *Post-it Notes* — for sticking your ideas to the page

3. *Bookmarks* — for marking your place when you need to boil water for another cup of tea

4. *Book darts* — for precise line marking and pretty page edges

5. *Dog-eared pages* — for loving your books well and revisiting favorite scenes

6. *Your favorite pencil* — for underlining quotes, ideas, and lightbulb moments

7. *Pastel highlighters* — for pretty but subtle annotations

8. *A fine-point pen* — for writing careful notes in the margins

9. *A book sleeve* — for protecting your current read from the elements

10. *A book cart* — for prioritizing your "to be read" piles and storing your reading tools

Title

AUTHOR: ....

GENRE: .... LENGTH: ....

PUBLISHER: .... YEAR PUBLISHED: ....

THEMES: ....

◇ FICTION

◇ NONFICTION

DATE STARTED

DATE FINISHED

HOW I DISCOVERED THIS BOOK:

MEMORABLE QUOTES:

My Ratings

◇◇◇◇◇
ENJOYMENT

◇◇◇◇◇
CRAFT

THOUGHTS & IMPRESSIONS:

◇◇◇◇◇
OVERALL

I'D RECOMMEND
THIS TO:

....
....
....
....

BOOK NO.

83

◇ FICTION
◇ NONFICTION

DATE STARTED

DATE FINISHED

My Ratings

◇◇◇◇◇
ENJOYMENT

◇◇◇◇◇
CRAFT

◇◇◇◇◇
OVERALL

I'D RECOMMEND
THIS TO:

Title

AUTHOR:

GENRE: LENGTH:

PUBLISHER: YEAR PUBLISHED:

THEMES:

HOW I DISCOVERED THIS BOOK:

MEMORABLE QUOTES:

THOUGHTS & IMPRESSIONS:

Title

AUTHOR: _____

GENRE: _____ LENGTH: _____

PUBLISHER: _____ YEAR PUBLISHED: _____

THEMES: _____

◇ FICTION

◇ NONFICTION

DATE STARTED

DATE FINISHED

HOW I DISCOVERED THIS BOOK:

MEMORABLE QUOTES:

My Ratings

◇◇◇◇◇
ENJOYMENT

◇◇◇◇◇
CRAFT

◇◇◇◇◇
OVERALL

THOUGHTS & IMPRESSIONS:

I'D RECOMMEND
THIS TO:

_____
_____
_____

BOOK NO.
85

◇ FICTION
◇ NONFICTION

DATE STARTED

DATE FINISHED

My Ratings

◇◇◇◇◇
ENJOYMENT

◇◇◇◇◇
CRAFT

◇◇◇◇◇
OVERALL

I'D RECOMMEND
THIS TO:

Title

AUTHOR:

GENRE: LENGTH:

PUBLISHER: YEAR PUBLISHED:

THEMES:

HOW I DISCOVERED THIS BOOK:

MEMORABLE QUOTES:

THOUGHTS & IMPRESSIONS:

Title

◇ FICTION
◇ NONFICTION

AUTHOR:

GENRE: LENGTH:

PUBLISHER: YEAR PUBLISHED:

THEMES:

DATE STARTED

DATE FINISHED

HOW I DISCOVERED THIS BOOK:

MEMORABLE QUOTES:

My Ratings

◇◇◇◇◇
ENJOYMENT

◇◇◇◇◇
CRAFT

◇◇◇◇◇
OVERALL

THOUGHTS & IMPRESSIONS:

I'D RECOMMEND
THIS TO:

*If you truly love a book,
you should sleep with it,
write in it, read aloud
from it, and fill its pages
with muffin crumbs.*

— Anne Fadiman

Title

AUTHOR:

GENRE: LENGTH:

PUBLISHER: YEAR PUBLISHED:

THEMES:

◇ FICTION
◇ NONFICTION

DATE STARTED

DATE FINISHED

HOW I DISCOVERED THIS BOOK:

MEMORABLE QUOTES:

My Ratings

◇◇◇◇◇
ENJOYMENT

◇◇◇◇◇
CRAFT

◇◇◇◇◇
OVERALL

THOUGHTS & IMPRESSIONS:

I'D RECOMMEND
THIS TO:

BOOK NO.

88

◇ FICTION
◇ NONFICTION

DATE STARTED

DATE FINISHED

My Ratings

◇◇◇◇◇
ENJOYMENT

◇◇◇◇◇
CRAFT

◇◇◇◇◇
OVERALL

I'D RECOMMEND
THIS TO:

Title

AUTHOR:

GENRE: LENGTH:

PUBLISHER: YEAR PUBLISHED:

THEMES:

HOW I DISCOVERED THIS BOOK:

MEMORABLE QUOTES:

THOUGHTS & IMPRESSIONS:

Title

AUTHOR: ....

GENRE: .... LENGTH: ....

PUBLISHER: .... YEAR PUBLISHED: ....

THEMES: ....

HOW I DISCOVERED THIS BOOK:

MEMORABLE QUOTES:

THOUGHTS & IMPRESSIONS:

◇ FICTION

◇ NONFICTION

DATE STARTED

DATE FINISHED

My Ratings

◇◇◇◇◇
ENJOYMENT

◇◇◇◇◇
CRAFT

◇◇◇◇◇
OVERALL

I'D RECOMMEND
THIS TO:

....

....

....

....

BOOK NO.

90

◇ FICTION
◇ NONFICTION

DATE STARTED

DATE FINISHED

My Ratings

◇◇◇◇◇
ENJOYMENT

◇◇◇◇◇
CRAFT

◇◇◇◇◇
OVERALL

I'D RECOMMEND
THIS TO:

Title

AUTHOR:

GENRE: LENGTH:

PUBLISHER: YEAR PUBLISHED:

THEMES:

HOW I DISCOVERED THIS BOOK:

MEMORABLE QUOTES:

THOUGHTS & IMPRESSIONS:

Title

AUTHOR: ....

GENRE: .... LENGTH: ....

PUBLISHER: .... YEAR PUBLISHED: ....

THEMES: ....

HOW I DISCOVERED THIS BOOK:

MEMORABLE QUOTES:

THOUGHTS & IMPRESSIONS:

◇ FICTION

◇ NONFICTION

DATE STARTED

DATE FINISHED

My Ratings

◇◇◇◇◇
ENJOYMENT

◇◇◇◇◇
CRAFT

◇◇◇◇◇
OVERALL

I'D RECOMMEND
THIS TO:

....
....
....
....

BOOK NO.

92

◇ FICTION
◇ NONFICTION

DATE STARTED

DATE FINISHED

My Ratings

◇◇◇◇◇
ENJOYMENT

◇◇◇◇◇
CRAFT

◇◇◇◇◇
OVERALL

I'D RECOMMEND
THIS TO:

Title

AUTHOR:

GENRE: LENGTH:

PUBLISHER: YEAR PUBLISHED:

THEMES:

HOW I DISCOVERED THIS BOOK:

MEMORABLE QUOTES:

THOUGHTS & IMPRESSIONS:

Title

AUTHOR: ....

GENRE: .... LENGTH: ....

PUBLISHER: .... YEAR PUBLISHED: ....

THEMES: ....

HOW I DISCOVERED THIS BOOK:

MEMORABLE QUOTES:

THOUGHTS & IMPRESSIONS:

◇ FICTION

◇ NONFICTION

DATE STARTED

DATE FINISHED

My Ratings

◇◇◇◇◇
ENJOYMENT

◇◇◇◇◇
CRAFT

◇◇◇◇◇
OVERALL

I'D RECOMMEND
THIS TO:

....
....
....
....

BOOK NO.

94

◇ FICTION
◇ NONFICTION

DATE STARTED

DATE FINISHED

My Ratings

◇◇◇◇◇
ENJOYMENT

◇◇◇◇◇
CRAFT

◇◇◇◇◇
OVERALL

I'D RECOMMEND
THIS TO:

Title

AUTHOR:

GENRE: LENGTH:

PUBLISHER: YEAR PUBLISHED:

THEMES:

HOW I DISCOVERED THIS BOOK:

MEMORABLE QUOTES:

THOUGHTS & IMPRESSIONS:

Title

AUTHOR: ....

GENRE: .... LENGTH: ....

PUBLISHER: .... YEAR PUBLISHED: ....

THEMES: ....

HOW I DISCOVERED THIS BOOK:

MEMORABLE QUOTES:

THOUGHTS & IMPRESSIONS:

◇ FICTION
◇ NONFICTION

DATE STARTED

DATE FINISHED

My Ratings

◇◇◇◇◇
ENJOYMENT

◇◇◇◇◇
CRAFT

◇◇◇◇◇
OVERALL

I'D RECOMMEND
THIS TO:

....

....

....

BOOK NO.

96

◇ FICTION
◇ NONFICTION

DATE STARTED

DATE FINISHED

My Ratings

◇◇◇◇◇
ENJOYMENT

◇◇◇◇◇
CRAFT

◇◇◇◇◇
OVERALL

I'D RECOMMEND
THIS TO:

Title

AUTHOR:

GENRE: LENGTH:

PUBLISHER: YEAR PUBLISHED:

THEMES:

HOW I DISCOVERED THIS BOOK:

MEMORABLE QUOTES:

THOUGHTS & IMPRESSIONS:

Title

AUTHOR: ....

GENRE: .... LENGTH: ....

PUBLISHER: .... YEAR PUBLISHED: ....

THEMES: ....

◇ FICTION

◇ NONFICTION

| / | / |

DATE STARTED

| / | / |

DATE FINISHED

HOW I DISCOVERED THIS BOOK:

MEMORABLE QUOTES:

My Ratings

◇◇◇◇◇
ENJOYMENT

◇◇◇◇◇
CRAFT

THOUGHTS & IMPRESSIONS:

◇◇◇◇◇
OVERALL

I'D RECOMMEND
THIS TO:

....

....

....

....

BOOK NO.

....

98

◇ FICTION
◇ NONFICTION

DATE STARTED

DATE FINISHED

My Ratings

◇◇◇◇◇
ENJOYMENT

◇◇◇◇◇
CRAFT

◇◇◇◇◇
OVERALL

I'D RECOMMEND
THIS TO:

Title

AUTHOR:

GENRE: LENGTH:

PUBLISHER: YEAR PUBLISHED:

THEMES:

HOW I DISCOVERED THIS BOOK:

MEMORABLE QUOTES:

THOUGHTS & IMPRESSIONS:

Title

AUTHOR: ....

GENRE: .... LENGTH: ....

PUBLISHER: .... YEAR PUBLISHED: ....

THEMES: ....

◇ FICTION

◇ NONFICTION

DATE STARTED

DATE FINISHED

HOW I DISCOVERED THIS BOOK:

MEMORABLE QUOTES:

My Ratings

◇◇◇◇◇
ENJOYMENT

◇◇◇◇◇
CRAFT

THOUGHTS & IMPRESSIONS:

◇◇◇◇◇
OVERALL

I'D RECOMMEND
THIS TO:

....
....
....
....

BOOK NO.
100

◇ FICTION
◇ NONFICTION

DATE STARTED

DATE FINISHED

My Ratings

◇◇◇◇◇
ENJOYMENT

◇◇◇◇◇
CRAFT

◇◇◇◇◇
OVERALL

I'D RECOMMEND
THIS TO:

Title

AUTHOR:

GENRE: LENGTH:

PUBLISHER: YEAR PUBLISHED:

THEMES:

HOW I DISCOVERED THIS BOOK:

MEMORABLE QUOTES:

THOUGHTS & IMPRESSIONS:

If a book is well written, I always find it too short.

— Jane Austen

More Book Lists

- WHAT SHOULD I READ NEXT? -

The following lists burst with bookish inspiration, including more than 200 enticing titles to broaden the scope and depth of your reading life.

COMPULSIVELY READABLE LITERARY FICTION

Combining the best of both worlds, these books are strong not only
on beautiful prose and interior characterization but also on plot.

◇   *Rules of Civility* | Amor Towles

◇   *Station Eleven* | Emily St. John Mandel

◇   *Let the Great World Spin* | Colum McCann

◇   *The Sellout* | Paul Beatty

◇   *Silver Sparrow* | Tayari Jones

◇   *This Is How It Always Is* | Laurie Frankel

◇   *We Are All Completely Beside Ourselves* | Karen Joy Fowler

◇   *The Mothers* | Brit Bennett

◇   *Montana 1948* | Larry Watson

◇   *Exit West* | Mohsin Hamid

◇   *Plainsong* | Kent Haruf

◇   *Stay with Me* | Ayobami Adebayo

◇   *This Must Be the Place* | Maggie O'Farrell

◇   *Home Fire* | Kamila Shamsie

◇   *Everything I Never Told You* | Celeste Ng

◇   *The Namesake* | Jhumpa Lahiri

◇   *A Place for Us* | Fatima Farheen Mirza

◇   *What We Were Promised* | Lucy Tan

◇   *The Dog Stars* | Peter Heller

◇   *The Dearly Beloved* | Cara Wall

CLASSICS YOU SHOULD HAVE READ IN HIGH SCHOOL THAT ARE WORTH READING NOW

Do you get a little panicky when you consider all the books you feel like you should have read by now? Take heart—you'll get more out of reading these books now than you ever would have gotten out of them in high school.

◇ *The Great Gatsby* | F. Scott Fitzgerald

◇ *Jane Eyre* | Charlotte Brontë

◇ *Mrs. Dalloway* | Virginia Woolf

◇ *I Know Why the Caged Bird Sings* | Maya Angelou

◇ *As I Lay Dying* | William Faulkner

◇ *East of Eden* | John Steinbeck

◇ *Passing* | Nella Larsen

◇ *David Copperfield* | Charles Dickens

◇ *Pride and Prejudice* | Jane Austen

◇ *To Kill a Mockingbird* | Harper Lee

◇ *Things Fall Apart* | Chinua Achebe

◇ *Their Eyes Were Watching God* | Zora Neale Hurston

◇ *Native Son* | Richard Wright

◇ *Fahrenheit 451* | Ray Bradbury

◇ *Invisible Man* | Ralph Ellison

◇ *Love in the Time of Cholera* | Gabriel García Márquez

◇ *Go Tell It on the Mountain* | James Baldwin

◇ *The Bluest Eye* | Toni Morrison

◇ *The Color Purple* | Alice Walker

◇ *The House of Mirth* | Edith Wharton

◇ *Frankenstein* | Mary Shelley

AUDIOBOOKS THAT ENHANCE THE READING EXPERIENCE

My favorite audiobooks are good for more than just hands-free reading while folding laundry or walking the dog. The best audiobooks aren't a substitute for actual books; rather, they enhance the reading experience by adding layers to it. *(Narrators are listed below after the authors.)*

◇ **The Jane Austen Society** | Natalie Jenner | *(Richard Armitage)*

◇ **The Dutch House** | Ann Patchett | *(Tom Hanks)*

◇ **Americanah** | Chimamanda Ngozi Adichie | *(Adjoa Andoh)*

◇ **This Tender Land** | William Kent Krueger | *(Scott Brick)*

◇ **On the Come Up** | Angie Thomas | *(Bahni Turpin)*

◇ **Magpie Murders** | Anthony Horowitz | *(Samantha Bond & Allan Corduner)*

◇ **Quick Service** | P.G. Wodehouse | *(Simon Vance)*

◇ **Echo** | Pam Muñoz Ryan | *(Mark Bramhall, David de Vries, Andrews MacLeod, & Rebecca Soler)*

◇ **The Good House** | Ann Leary | *(Mary Beth Hurt)*

◇ **A Prayer for Owen Meany** | John Irving | *(Joe Barrett)*

◇ **The Handmaid's Tale** | Margaret Atwood | *(Claire Danes)*

◇ **The End of the Affair** | Graham Greene | *(Colin Firth)*

◇ **The Watsons Go to Birmingham** | Christopher Paul Curtis | *(LeVar Burton)*

◇ **Daisy Jones and the Six** | Taylor Jenkins Reid | *(Jennifer Beals, Benjamin Bratt, Judy Greet, and Pablo Schreiber)*

◇ **Pride: A Pride and Prejudice Remix** | Ibi Zoboi | *(Elizabeth Acevedo)*

◇ **Nothing to See Here** | Kevin Wilson | *(Marin Ireland)*

◇ **The Stationery Shop** | Marjan Kamali | *(Mozhan Marnò)*

◇ **The Song of Achilles** | Madeline Miller | *(Frazer Douglas)*

◇ **Lovely War** | Julie Berry | *(Julie Berry, Jayne Entwistle, Allan Corduner, Dion Graham, Fiona Hardingham, John Lee, Nathaniel Parker, & Steve West)*

◇ **Before the Ever After** | Jacqueline Woodson | *(Guy Lockardt)*

SPIRITUAL MEMOIR & BIOGRAPHY

As a naturally introspective reader, I enjoy this genre for its thought-provoking themes and soul-stirring stories. Some of these books have shaped my own faith journey; others have given me a window into the spiritual lives of others.

◇ *Walking on Water* | Madeleine L'Engle

◇ *Take This Bread* | Sara Miles

◇ *The Seven Storey Mountain* | Thomas Merton

◇ *Muslim Girl* | Amani al-Khatahtbeh

◇ *Searching for Sunday* | Rachel Held Evans

◇ *The Hiding Place* | Corrie ten Boom with Elizabeth & John Sherrill

◇ *Learning to Walk in the Dark* | Barbara Brown Taylor

◇ *Ordinary Light* | Tracy K. Smith

◇ *The Cost of Discipleship* | Dietrich Bonhoeffer

◇ *All Is Grace* | Brennan Manning

◇ *The Divine Conspiracy* | Dallas Willard

◇ *Surprised by Oxford* | Carolyn Weber

◇ *Miracles and Other Reasonable Things* | Sarah Bessey

◇ *The Eyes of the Heart* | Frederick Buechner

◇ *Surprised by Joy* | C.S. Lewis

◇ *Story of a Soul* | Thérèse de Lisieux

◇ *The Return of the Prodigal Son* | Henri J.M. Nouwen

◇ *With Head and Heart* | Howard Thurman

◇ *The Simple Faith of Mr. Rogers* | Amy Hollingsworth

◇ *Native* | Kaitlin B. Curtice

LIFE-CHANGING NONFICTION BOOKS SHORT ENOUGH TO FINISH IN A DAY

At two hundred pages or less, readers can knock off one of these slim works in an afternoon. Whether you choose a book about racism, houseplants, productivity, or science, you'll think about what you read long after you finish.

◇ *Help, Thanks, Wow* | Anne Lamott

◇ *I'm Still Here* | Austin Channing Brown

◇ *The War of Art* | Steven Pressfield

◇ *What the Most Successful People Do Before Breakfast* | Laura Vanderkam

◇ *The Quotidian Mysteries* | Kathleen Norris

◇ *Between the World and Me* | Ta-Nehisi Coates

◇ *You Learn by Living* | Eleanor Roosevelt

◇ *The Little Book of Talent* | Daniel Coyle

◇ *The Alchemist* | Paulo Coelho

◇ *One Small Step Can Change Your Life* | Robert Maurer

◇ *A Room of One's Own* | Virginia Woolf

◇ *The Fire Next Time* | James Baldwin

◇ *We Should All Be Feminists* | Chimamanda Ngozi Adichie

◇ *Zen in the Art of Writing* | Ray Bradbury

◇ *Tell Me More* | Kelly Corrigan

◇ *The Elements of Style* | William Strunk Jr. & E.B. White

◇ *Reading People* | Anne Bogel

◇ *The Diving Bell and the Butterfly* | Jean-Dominique Bauby

◇ *A Briefer History of Time* | Stephen Hawking with Leonard Mlodinow

◇ *The Origin of Others* | Toni Morrison

EXTRA-LONG BOOKS

These towering tomes are worth tackling. With an average of six hundred pages per book, these well-loved favorites will last you a while or help you get the most out of your audiobook credits.

◇ *Wives and Daughters* | Elizabeth Gaskell

◇ *The Stand* | Stephen King

◇ *Alexander Hamilton* | Ron Chernow

◇ *The Count of Monte Cristo* | Alexandre Dumas

◇ *Middlemarch* | George Eliot

◇ *Angle of Repose* | Wallace Stegner

◇ *A Tree Grows in Brooklyn* | Betty Smith

◇ *A Discovery of Witches* | Deborah Harkness

◇ *The Fifth Season* | N.K. Jemisin

◇ *Resistance Women* | Jennifer Chiaverini

◇ *Centennial* | James A. Michener

◇ *I Know This Much Is True* | Wally Lamb

◇ *In This House of Brede* | Rumer Godden

◇ *A Suitable Boy* | Vikram Seth

◇ *Kristin Lavransdatter* | Sigrid Undset

◇ *Half of a Yellow Sun* | Chimamanda Ngozi Adichie

◇ *Here Be Dragons* | Sharon Kay Penman

◇ *A Brief History of Seven Killings* | Marlon James

◇ *The Weight of Ink* | Rachel Kadish

◇ *A Fine Balance* | Rohinton Mistry

FEEL-GOOD FICTION

I love these books because while they feel light and easy, they have serious substance beneath the surface. Memorable characters and poignant themes will linger long after you turn the final page.

◇ *What Alice Forgot* | Liane Moriarty
◇ *Far from the Tree* | Robin Benway
◇ *The Lost Husband* | Katherine Center
◇ *You Should See Me in a Crown* | Leah Johnson
◇ *Love Walked In* | Marisa de los Santos
◇ *The House in the Cerulean Sea* | TJ Klune
◇ *The Bookshop on the Corner* | Jenny Colgan
◇ *Piecing Me Together* | Renée Watson
◇ *Less* | Andrew Sean Greer
◇ *Evvie Drake Starts Over* | Linda Holmes
◇ *The One-in-a-Million Boy* | Monica Wood
◇ *The Garden of Small Beginnings* | Abbi Waxman
◇ *Ayesha at Last* | Uzma Jalaluddin
◇ *Harry's Trees* | Jon Cohen
◇ *The Rosie Project* | Graeme Simsion
◇ *The Wedding Date* | Jasmine Guillory
◇ *Auntie Poldi and the Sicilian Lions* | Mario Giordano
◇ *Tweet Cute* | Emma Lord
◇ *How to Stop Time* | Matt Haig
◇ *The Lager Queen of Minnesota* | J. Ryan Stradal

FOOD MEMOIRS

Food is full of stories, from the family history behind a handed-down dish to juicy kitchen drama at a high-end restaurant to the culinary embodiment of a culture's roots and traditions. Even if you don't love to cook, certainly you'll enjoy one of these great stories, well told.

◇ *A Homemade Life* | Molly Wizenberg

◇ *Garlic and Sapphires* | Ruth Reichl

◇ *The Sweet Life in Paris* | David Lebovitz

◇ *My Life in France* | Julia Child with Alex Prud'homme

◇ *The Kitchen Counter Cooking School* | Kathleen Flinn

◇ *Home Cooking* | Laurie Colwin

◇ *Mastering the Art of French Eating* | Ann Mah

◇ *Yes, Chef* | Marcus Samuelsson with Veronica Chambers

◇ *Blood, Bones & Butter* | Gabrielle Hamilton

◇ *From Scratch* | Tembi Locke

◇ *Bread and Wine* | Shauna Niequist

◇ *The Cooking Gene* | Michael W. Twitty

◇ *Dirt* | Bill Buford

◇ *The Comfort Food Diaries* | Emily Nunn

◇ *The Language of Baklava* | Diana Abu-Jaber

◇ *The Dirty Life* | Kristin Kimball

◇ *Notes from a Young Black Chef* | Kwame Onwuachi with Joshua David Stein

◇ *Stir* | Jessica Fechtor

◇ *Orchard House* | Tara Austen Weaver

◇ *Climbing the Mango Trees* | Madhur Jaffrey

BOOKS TO TAKE YOU AROUND THE WORLD

With a good book, carefully chosen, you can take a grand adventure
without leaving the comfy chair in your living room. Enjoy some
armchair travel with these books set around the globe.

◇ *Cutting for Stone* | Abraham Verghese | *(India, Ethiopia, and USA)*

◇ *Daughter of Smoke and Bone* | Laini Taylor | *(Prague)*

◇ *Faithful Place* | Tana French | *(Dublin)*

◇ *Strange Weather in Tokyo* | Hiromi Kawakami | *(Tokyo)*

◇ *State of Wonder* | Ann Patchett | *(USA, Brazil)*

◇ *Four Seasons in Rome* | Anthony Doerr | *(Italy)*

◇ *A Gentleman in Moscow* | Amor Towles | *(Moscow)*

◇ *The Year of Living Danishly* | Helen Russell | *(Denmark)*

◇ *The Fishermen* | Chigozie Obioma | *(Nigeria)*

◇ *Next Year in Havana* | Chanel Cleeton | *(Cuba)*

◇ *The Shadow of the Wind* | Carlos Ruiz Zafón | *(Madrid)*

◇ *The Luminaries* | Eleanor Catton | *(New Zealand)*

◇ *No Knives in the Kitchens of This City* | Khaled Khalifa | *(Aleppo)*

◇ *All the Light We Cannot See* | Anthony Doerr | *(Essen, Paris, and Saint-Malo)*

◇ *The Historian* | Elizabeth Kostova | *(the Netherlands, England, France, Croatia Bulgaria, Hungary, and Turkey)*

◇ *The Survivors* | Jane Harper | *(Tasmania)*

◇ *Crazy Rich Asians* | Kevin Kwan | *(USA and Singapore)*

◇ *The Boat People* | Sharon Bala | *(British Columbia and Sri Lanka)*

◇ *Clap When You Land* | Elizabeth Acevedo | *(NYC and the Dominican Republic)*

◇ *Don't Let's Go to the Dogs Tonight* | Alexandra Fuller | *(Rhodesia, Malawi, and Zambia)*

BOOKS ABOUT BOOKS & BOOKSTORES

A good story is an experience, and many of us enjoy the extra layer of bibliophile enjoyment provided by a book about a book, or that takes place in a bookstore. There's something for everyone here: literary mystery, bookstore memoir, love stories, heartwarming correspondence, treacherous librarians. The deep love of reading unites them all.

◇ *The Storied Life of A.J. Fikry* | Gabrielle Zevin
◇ *Parnassus on Wheels* | Christopher Morley
◇ *Escaping Dreamland* | Charlie Lovett
◇ *I'd Rather Be Reading* | Anne Bogel
◇ *The End of Your Life Book Club* | Will Schwalbe
◇ *The Brontë Plot* | Katherine Reay
◇ *The Library Book* | Susan Orlean
◇ *The Word Exchange* | Alena Graedon
◇ *84, Charing Cross Road* | Helene Hanff
◇ *Ink and Bone* | Rachel Caine
◇ *The Diary of a Bookseller* | Shaun Bythell
◇ *The Invisible Library* | Genevieve Cogman
◇ *How to Find Love in a Bookshop* | Veronica Henry
◇ *Possession* | A.S. Byatt
◇ *The Clothing of Books* | Jhumpa Lahiri
◇ *Mr. Penumbra's 24-Hour Bookstore* | Robin Sloan
◇ *Words in Deep Blue* | Cath Crowley
◇ *An Unnecessary Woman* | Rabih Alameddine
◇ *The Uncommon Reader* | Alan Bennett
◇ *The Secret, Book & Scone Society* | Ellery Adams

BOOKSTORES & OTHER LITERARY DESTINATIONS I'D LIKE TO VISIT

What a joy to browse the shelves of a well-stocked independent bookstore! A good indie thoroughly represents its community, which means when you visit a new one you're bound to come away with great book recommendations and a few great new (or new-to-you) titles for your "to be read" list.

AUDIOBOOKS NARRATED BY THE AUTHOR

Audiobooks are only as good as their narrators, and who better to bring a book to life than the author? These are some of my favorite audiobooks narrated by the authors themselves.

- ◇ *Born a Crime* | Trevor Noah
- ◇ *Dream More* | Dolly Parton
- ◇ *Becoming* | Michelle Obama
- ◇ *Kitchen Confidential* | Anthony Bourdain
- ◇ *Bossypants* | Tina Fey
- ◇ *Redwall* | Brian Jacques
- ◇ *Bird by Bird* | Anne Lamott
- ◇ *A Walk in the Woods* | Bill Bryson
- ◇ *Between, Georgia* | Joshilyn Jackson
- ◇ *The Poet X* | Elizabeth Acevedo
- ◇ *Swing* | Kwame Alexander
- ◇ *Long Way Down* | Jason Reynolds
- ◇ *Born Standing Up* | Steve Martin
- ◇ *Why Not Me?* | Mindy Kaling
- ◇ *Angela's Ashes* | Frank McCourt
- ◇ *Flight Behavior* | Barbara Kingsolver
- ◇ *My Southern Journey* | Rick Bragg
- ◇ *Beloved* | Toni Morrison
- ◇ *Calypso* | David Sedaris
- ◇ *LaRose* | Louise Erdich

RIVETING MYSTERIES

When you're hooked on a series, you're never in want of a good book to read next. With one exception (noted below), the first book of each series is listed, along with the name of the series.

◇ **A Great Deliverance** | Elizabeth George | *(Inspector Lynley)*

◇ **The Widows of Malabar Hill** | Sujata Massey | *(Perveen Mistry)*

◇ **A Share in Death** | Deborah Crombie | *(Duncan Kincaid/Gemma James)*

◇ **A Study in Scarlet Women** | Sherry Thomas | *(Lady Sherlock)*

◇ **Iron Lake** | William Kent Krueger | *(Cork O'Connor)*

◇ **A Is for Alibi** | Sue Grafton | *(Kinsey Millhone)*

◇ **The Calculating Stars** | Mary Robinette Kowal | *(Lady Astronaut)*

◇ **Still Life** | Louise Penny | *(Chief Inspector Gamache)*

◇ **A Rising Man** | Abir Mukherjee | *(Wyndham & Banerjee)*

◇ **Trouble Is a Friend of Mine** | Stephanie Tromly | *(Trouble)*

◇ **Death at La Fenice** | Donna Leon | *(Commissario Brunetti)*

◇ **The Eyre Affair** | Jasper Fforde | *(Thursday Next)*

◇ **Maisie Dobbs** | Jacqueline Winspear | *(Maisie Dobbs)*

◇ **In the Bleak Midwinter** | Julia Spencer-Fleming | *(Clare Fergusson/ Russ Van Alstyne)*

◇ **The Redbreast** | Jo Nesbø | *(Harry Hole book 3)*

◇ **Her Royal Spyness** | Rhys Bowen | *(Royal Spyness)*

◇ **Hollywood Homicide** | Kellye Garrett | *(Detective by Day)*

◇ **The No. 1 Ladies' Detective Agency** | Alexander McCall Smith | *(No. 1 Ladies' Detective Agency)*

◇ **Case Histories** | Kate Atkinson | *(Jackson Brodie)*

◇ **Knots and Crosses** | Ian Rankin | *(Inspector Rebus)*

BOOKS IN TRANSLATION

Good books help us empathize with and understand other people and cultures. When we read only books written in our own language, we miss a crucial opportunity. Expand your literary horizons with these books originally written in a language other than English.

◇ *The Time in Between* | Maria Dueñas | *(Spanish)*

◇ *Anna Karenina* | Leo Tolstoy | *(Russian)*

◇ *The Little Prince* | Antoine de Saint-Exupéry | *(French)*

◇ *Murmur of Bees* | Sofia Segovia | *(Spanish)*

◇ *The Elegance of the Hedgehog* | Muriel Barbery | *(French)*

◇ *My Brilliant Friend* | Elena Ferrante | *(Italian)*

◇ *Inkheart* | Cornelia Funke | *(German)*

◇ *1Q84* | Haruki Murakami | *(Japanese)*

◇ *A Man Called Ove* | Fredrik Backman | *(Swedish)*

◇ *Disoriental* | Négar Djavadi | *(French)*

◇ *The Vegetarian: A Novel* | Han Kang | *(Korean)*

◇ *Seven Brief Lessons on Physics* | Carlo Rovelli | *(Italian)*

◇ *The Big Green Tent* | Ludmila Ulitskaya | *(Russian)*

◇ *The History of Bees* | Maja Lunde | *(Norwegian)*

◇ *Convenience Store Woman* | Sayaka Murata | *(Japanese)*

◇ *War and Peace* | Leo Tolstoy | *(Russian)*

◇ *Night* | Elie Wiesel | *(Yiddish)*

◇ *The Mystery of Henri Pick* | David Foenkinos | *(French)*

◇ *Before the Coffee Gets Cold* | Toshikazu Kawaguchi | *(Japanese)*

◇ *Celestial Bodies* | Jokha Alharthi | *(Arabic)*

The *best*
candy shop
a child can be
left alone in is
the *library.*

— Maya Angelou

Favorites & Other Logs

- FAVORITE BOOKS -

My reading life is one of my deepest pleasures.

»» ——» YAA GYASI «—— ««

The wise man reads both books and life itself.

≫⟶≫   LIN YUTANG   ≪⟵≪

- FAVORITE QUOTES -

Wear the old coat and buy the new book.

≫——≫   AUSTIN PHELPS   ≪——≪

- FAVORITE QUOTES -

Some say life is the thing, but I prefer reading.

➤➤➤ ➤➤ RUTH RENDELL ⪻ ⪻⪻

- BOOKS I'VE BORROWED OR LOANED -

TITLE: ....   DATE: ....

FROM / TO : ....   ◇ RETURNED

TITLE: ....   DATE: ....

FROM / TO : ....   ◇ RETURNED

TITLE: ....   DATE: ....

FROM / TO : ....   ◇ RETURNED

TITLE: ....   DATE: ....

FROM / TO : ....   ◇ RETURNED

TITLE: ....   DATE: ....

FROM / TO : ....   ◇ RETURNED

TITLE: ....   DATE: ....

FROM / TO : ....   ◇ RETURNED

TITLE: ....   DATE: ....

FROM / TO : ....   ◇ RETURNED

TITLE: DATE:

FROM / TO : ◇ RETURNED

TITLE: DATE:

FROM / TO : ◇ RETURNED

TITLE: DATE:

FROM / TO : ◇ RETURNED

TITLE: DATE:

FROM / TO : ◇ RETURNED

TITLE: DATE:

FROM / TO : ◇ RETURNED

TITLE: DATE:

FROM / TO : ◇ RETURNED

TITLE: DATE:

FROM / TO : ◇ RETURNED

TITLE: DATE:

FROM / TO : ◇ RETURNED

TITLE: DATE:

FROM / TO : ◇ RETURNED

- BOOKS I'VE GIVEN/RECEIVED AS GIFTS -

TITLE: _____ DATE: _____

GIVEN TO / RECEIVED FROM: _____

OCCASION: _____

TITLE: _____ DATE: _____

GIVEN TO / RECEIVED FROM: _____

OCCASION: _____

TITLE: _____ DATE: _____

GIVEN TO / RECEIVED FROM: _____

OCCASION: _____

TITLE: _____ DATE: _____

GIVEN TO / RECEIVED FROM: _____

OCCASION: _____

TITLE: _____ DATE: _____

GIVEN TO / RECEIVED FROM: _____

OCCASION: _____

TITLE: _____ DATE: _____

GIVEN TO / RECEIVED FROM: _____

OCCASION: _____

TITLE: _____ DATE: _____

GIVEN TO / RECEIVED FROM: _____

OCCASION: _____

TITLE: _____ DATE: _____

GIVEN TO / RECEIVED FROM: _____

OCCASION: _____

TITLE: _____ DATE: _____

GIVEN TO / RECEIVED FROM: _____

OCCASION: _____

TITLE: _____ DATE: _____

GIVEN TO / RECEIVED FROM: _____

OCCASION: _____

TITLE: _____ DATE: _____

GIVEN TO / RECEIVED FROM: _____

OCCASION: _____

TITLE: _____ DATE: _____

GIVEN TO / RECEIVED FROM: _____

OCCASION: _____

TITLE: _____ DATE: _____

GIVEN TO / RECEIVED FROM: _____

OCCASION: _____

Reflecting on My Reading Year

A new discovery I've made about my reading life is

_____

_____

_____

_____

_____

A reading achievement I'm especially proud of is

_____

_____

_____

_____

As a reader, I've gained confidence in

_____

_____

_____

_____

A book that really surprised me this year is

_____

_____

_____

_____

_____

Someone I'd like to thank for their contribution to my reading life is

_____

_____

_____

_____

Something I've changed my mind about in the reading life is

_____

_____

_____

_____

Something I want more of in my reading life is

_____

_____

_____

_____

- FAVORITE BOOKS OF THE YEAR -

1. ....

2. ....

3. ....

4. ....

5. ....

6. ....

7. ....

8. ....

9. ....

10. ....

FAVORITE FICTION

FAVORITE NONFICTION

Conclusion

When you get more out of your reading life, your whole life benefits. Time spent reading and reflecting on the books we love is time well spent.

It's each reader's pleasure and privilege to build her own reading life, and we do that one book at a time. You've used this journal to record 100 books you've read, give or take a few. How have those books changed you as a reader?

I hope the books you've recorded here, the experiences you've enjoyed, and the reflections you've engaged in have made you a more empowered reader—one who is more at ease in her own reading life, more conversant about the books she loves (and doesn't), and quicker to identify why a book is working for her (or isn't).

Index

BOOK LISTS

📖 FEATURES

LOGS & OTHER PERSONAL NOTES

About the Author

Anne Bogel is an author, the creator of the blog *Modern Mrs Darcy*, host of the *What Should I Read Next?* and *One Great Book* podcasts, and an unabashed bibliophile.

Her other books include *Don't Overthink It*, *Reading People*, and *I'd Rather Be Reading*.

Anne's popular blog *Modern Mrs Darcy*, which derives its name from a Jane Austen book, is a lifestyle blog for nerds who appreciate Anne's modus operandi of approaching old, familiar ideas from new and fresh angles. While *Modern Mrs Darcy* isn't strictly a book blog, Anne writes frequently about books and reading. Her book lists are among her most popular posts. She is well known by readers, authors, and publishers as a tastemaker.

In 2016, she launched her podcast *What Should I Read Next?*—a popular show devoted to literary matchmaking, bibliotherapy, and all things books and reading. Her second podcast *One Great Book* launched in 2019. In the *Modern Mrs Darcy Book Club*, she helps people learn to read better, together.

Anne and all her books reside in Louisville, Kentucky, sharing space with her husband, four children, and a yellow Lab named Daisy.

For more from Anne, visit ModernMrsDarcy.com.

Cover Design by Faceout Studio
Interior design by Leah Beachy
Cover and interior background patterns © Anugraha Design / Creative Market

Published in association with William K. Jensen Literary Agency, 119 Bampton
Court, Eugene, Oregon 97404.

Ten Peaks Press is a trademark of The Hawkins Children's LLC. Harvest House
Publishers, Inc., is the exclusive licensee of the trademark Ten Peaks Press.

My Reading Life

Copyright © 2021 by Anne Bogel
Published by Ten Peaks Press, an imprint of Harvest House Publishers
Eugene, Oregon 97408

ISBN 978-0-7369-8302-0 (hardcover)

Printed in China

22 23 24 25 26 27 28 29 / RDS / 10 9 8 7 6 5 4 3